THE PLEA

IOWA AND THE MIDWEST EXPERIENCE

Series editor, William B. Friedricks,

Iowa History Center at Simpson College

THE PLEA

The True Story of
Young Wesley Elkins and
His Struggle for Redemption

Patricia L. Bryan
and Thomas Wolf

UNIVERSITY OF IOWA PRESS, IOWA CITY

University of Iowa Press, Iowa City 52242
Copyright © 2022 by Patricia L. Bryan and Thomas Wolf
uipress.uiowa.edu
Printed in the United States of America

Printed on acid-free paper

Library of Congress Cataloging-in-Publication Data
Names: Bryan, Patricia L., 1951– author. | Wolf, Thomas, 1947– author.
Title: The Plea: The True Story of Young Wesley Elkins and His
Struggle for Redemption / by Patricia L. Bryan and Thomas Wolf.
Description: Iowa City: University of Iowa Press, [2022] | Series: Iowa
and the Midwest experience | Includes bibliographical references. |
Identifiers: LCCN 2021054794 (print) | LCCN 2021054795 (ebook) |
ISBN 9781609388393 (paperback) | ISBN 9781609388409 (ebook)
Subjects: LCSH: Elkins, John Wesley, 1879–1961—Trials,
litigation, etc. | Elkins, John Wesley, 1879–1961—Pardon. |
Juvenile homicide—Iowa—History—nineteenth century. |
Patricide—Iowa—History—nineteenth century.
Classification: LCC KF223.E428 B79 2022 (print) | LCC KF223.
E428 (ebook) | DDC 345.777/02523—dc23/eng/20220202
LC record available at https://lccn.loc.gov/2021054794
LC ebook record available at https://lccn.loc.gov/2021054795

For our sons

John Benjamin Wolf

Michael Bryan Wolf

David Bryan Wolf

And for

Steve Wendl and Richard Snavely (1946–2018)

Who told us the story of John Wesley Elkins

TO THE READER

THIS BOOK STARTS with a terrible crime. The story is true. None of the characters are invented. All the scenes derive from primary sources—newspaper reports, legal documents, interviews, nonfiction works, memoirs, letters—and we quote from these materials throughout the narrative.

When it seemed appropriate, we have speculated on certain events and indicated where there is a gap in the historical record. This occurs mostly in the final chapters of the book. The reader will find information about our sources in the bibliography.

The central figure in this story is John Wesley Elkins, who was born near Elkader, Iowa. The exact date of his birth cannot be confirmed. We have not found a birth certificate and doubt that one was ever recorded. Elkins sometimes claimed July 12, 1878, as his birthdate, so for the purposes of this narrative, we have accepted that as the day and year of his birth.

For more than a dozen years, the fate of Wesley Elkins was in the hands of others, including legal authorities, journalists, educators, and politicians. His story captured the attention of a divided and transfixed public, raising questions about the criminal justice system and the rights of children. Ultimately, his destiny was determined by Iowa legislators during several days of heated public debate in the gold-domed capitol building in Des Moines, Iowa.

When Elkins died in California in 1961, a short obituary appeared in the *San Bernardino Sun*. Nothing in the death notice suggested the drama and turmoil of his early life. There was no mention of his decade-long legal struggle or how he lived his life as an adult. There was just the simple acknowledgment that in his last years he worked as a poultry farmer.

After the turbulent years of his youth, Elkins sought—and largely found—a kind of anonymity. In truth, he had no desire for this story to be told.

THE CRIME
1889

1.

ON WEDNESDAY, July 17, 1889, John Porter, a sixty-one-year-old Iowa farmer, stood in the yard outside his farmhouse just as the sun was rising. He looked out at his fields, 120 acres of fertile and undulating Iowa farmland. He already sensed it would be a brutally hot day.

In the thirty-six years Porter had owned this land, where he lived with his wife and two adult sons, he couldn't recall a heat spell much worse than this one. Despite the weather, Iowa farmers were enjoying a good summer, and Porter was pleased with his crops. The fields of barley and wheat were mostly harvested, and the harvest of oats was underway. The sweltering heat seemed to accelerate the growth of the corn crop that blanketed much of Porter's land and was now nearly as tall as a man.

As the sky lightened, Porter's reverie was interrupted by the clatter of a one-horse buggy coming down the dirt road that passed in front of his house. Porter saw the horse first, and then the buggy came into view. A child was sitting high on the wooden seat, holding the reins.

Porter recognized the boy as Wesley Elkins, the eleven-year-old son of his neighbor, John Elkins. Porter was well acquainted with Elkins, who owned and operated a local sawmill on the banks of Bear Creek, a tributary of the Iowa River. Elkins, who was forty-three years old, rented a house across from the mill on the outskirts of Porter's land. He lived there with his third wife, Hattie, twenty-three years old; their one-year-old daughter, Nellie; and Wesley, John's son from a previous marriage.

As the buggy approached the gate to his yard, Porter shouted to the boy, motioning for him to stop. Porter opened the gate, and Wesley steered the buggy up to the house and brought the horse to a halt. Wesley was wearing work clothes—overalls and a striped shirt. Although the sun was barely up, the boy had a dirty white felt hat pulled low over his eyes. As Porter stepped closer, he could see an infant, tightly wrapped in a blanket, lying on the wooden seat next to Wesley.

When Porter asked Wesley where he was headed, Wesley responded that he was taking the baby to Hattie's parents, the Outcalts, who lived a few miles away. Then he needed to fetch his older brother, Mark, who was boarding at the Woodall farm nearby. In a quiet voice, Wesley said that he had to tell Mark that their father and stepmother had been killed by an intruder a few hours earlier. Wesley didn't know who had done it, but he had seen their bodies in the bedroom, and he was sure they were dead.

Porter could hardly believe what he heard, but he didn't ask questions. He told Wesley to leave the baby with him and drive immediately to get Mark. Wesley nodded, and he lifted the baby and handed her out to Porter. As the boy leaned forward, Porter saw that Wesley's face and shirt were spotted with dark red flecks that looked like dried blood.

With the baby in his arms, Porter watched Wesley turn the horse around and drive the buggy through the gate out to the road. Wesley stopped briefly, and, when he climbed down from his perch and walked back to close the heavy gate behind him, Porter noticed that the boy was barefoot. Wesley returned to his seat, and the buggy continued down the dirt road, receding into the distance.

JOHN PORTER hurried inside to wake his family and tell them about his conversation with Wesley. Porter and his twenty-four-year-old son, George, agreed that they had to investigate.

Leaving the baby at the house with Porter's wife, Harriet, father and son made their way along the narrow road to the Elkins house about three-quarters of a mile away. The land was hilly with cultivated fields of oats and corn separated by patches of dense woods. The path twisted through a stand of trees, and the thick branches overhead blocked the early morning light. Bear Creek flowed nearby.

Porter knew this road well; he had visited John Elkins just the day before. Porter had an injured hand and hadn't been able to work in the fields that day, so he decided to inspect his crops. In the late afternoon, he paid a visit to his tenants. He found Elkins at his sewing machine, mending some clothes. The two men walked outside and then strolled through the oats and down to the spring. Porter remembered that he and Elkins sat on a fence, talking and joking together until dusk approached. They parted at the barnyard gate, going their separate ways. Porter hadn't noticed anything in his neighbor's manner suggesting that he was upset or worried.

Less than twelve hours later, Porter was again approaching the Elkins house, which stood isolated on top of a small rise. From a distance, nothing looked unusual. The barn, about 250 feet northwest of the house, was on lower ground and mostly hidden from view. It was larger than the house, with enough space for Elkins to keep his animals: two horses, a milk cow, a steer, and a calf. An ill-tempered dog often roamed about the property, but he was nowhere in sight. As a reporter for the local newspaper later wrote, the Elkins house was "favorably located for the commission of a terrible crime" since "no sounds or screams would reach the ears of those in the valley below."

The men called out as they got closer. When no one responded, they knocked and then tried to open the front door. It was locked, so they went around to the back; that door yielded to their touch and opened.

The house was small, 16 feet by 20 feet, with only three rooms. The men entered the largest one, which was sparsely furnished with a table and chairs, a chest with a clock on it, a cookstove, and the sewing machine where John Elkins had worked just the day before. Along the wall were doors to the two bedrooms, each about 8 feet by 9 feet, and barely large enough to fit a bed and a chest. Those doors were ajar, and taking only a few steps, the men could see inside the room that John and Hattie occupied.

The thin curtains at the window were drawn closed, and the room was in half-darkness. The men could just make out a grisly tableau on the double bed, less than two feet from where they stood.

The still form of Hattie, clad in a short nightshirt, was bent backward across the bed in an unnatural position, with her face toward the ceiling and her feet on the floor. Her features were disfigured, and her skull was broken open. The top half of her body partially covered her husband, who was also motionless, with his head turned to the side and resting on a pillow. He looked as if he were sleeping, but his face was destroyed. When Porter drew closer, he could see a bloody hole where the left eye should have been, and he figured that Elkins had been shot. Blood soaked the bedclothes and was spattered on the walls and the ceiling. There was a pool of the dark liquid by the bed, and Porter could see that someone had stood there and then walked barefoot to the door. A single track of bloody footprints marked the path.

Porter drew close enough to be sure the two were dead, and then he turned to the adjacent bedroom. It had a small bed—big enough for only one person—and the bedclothes were disturbed and spotted with blood. There was a single-barrel rifle hanging by two leather straps at the foot of the bed, and a small chest nearby. A lamp, a powder horn with its stopper out, and a few bullets lay on top of the chest. Porter stepped into the room and briefly inspected the rifle. When he hit the muzzle against the floor, some grains of powder came out, but no bullet had been loaded into the chamber. It looked to Porter as if someone had started to load the rifle and was interrupted in the task. He couldn't imagine that Elkins would have left his rifle in that condition.

Porter and his son talked briefly outside. They agreed that John Porter would stay with the bodies while his son alerted the community and reported the murders to the authorities.

BY MID-MORNING, the sun was high and the temperature already close to 90 degrees; the day would be recorded as one of the hottest of the summer. More than a dozen neighbors gathered at the Elkins house. A man named Ben Smith stood guard at the door, allowing only a select few to enter the house. The others clustered around the bedroom window, crushing a bed of morning glories and ripping the vines that grew up the outside wall. People took turns leaning their heads inside, pushing the curtains away to get a better view of the bodies on the bed.

The shocking news of what had happened at the Elkins farm spread quickly across the county. In Elkader, the county seat, Sheriff J. J. Kann was notified. Kann and his deputy, L. C. Place, started on their way to the crime scene, a distance of twelve miles. The two officials were accompanied by George Fairfield, publisher and editor of the *Elkader Register*.

Mark Elkins arrived at the house as the authorities were traveling there. Mark was twenty-one years old and Wesley's half-brother; they were both sons of John Elkins: Mark by his first wife, Phoebe, and Wesley by his second wife, Matilda. Mark told neighbors that he had gone to sleep in his rented room at W. G. Woodall's house when he was awakened by Wesley shouting in the window from the porch that their father and stepmother had been killed. Mr. Woodall heard the noise and came outside to question Wesley, who repeated what he had said: their father had been shot, and their stepmother "pounded to death." Wesley said he had been sleeping in the barn when it happened; he didn't know anything except that they were dead. Woodall and Mark were both dumbfounded by the news and wondered whether the story could be true.

Mark dressed quickly and drove himself and Wesley in the buggy back to the Porters. He left Wesley there, telling him to wait until his return. When Mark arrived at his father's house, the neighbors in the yard could see he was distraught. Ben Smith, still guarding the door, confirmed that it looked like murder, and he stood aside so Mark could see for himself. But Mark refused to go inside, saying he couldn't bear to lay eyes on the bloody bedroom or the dead bodies. He stayed for less than an hour, and then returned to the Porters to retrieve Wesley. He knew the sheriff would want to question his brother.

SHERIFF KANN and the other two men reached the house in mid-afternoon and went inside together. Fairfield later reported to his readers that the bloody bedroom presented "a scene that tried the nerves of the strongest." Sheriff Kann took a quick inventory of the rooms. He found $63.27 in cash in the bottom drawer of the chest, and he took that and the rifle hanging from the wall to hold as evidence. He later concluded that nothing of value appeared to be missing, and there was no evidence of a break-in.

Fairfield volunteered to search the yard. Before long, he discovered a club hidden under a pile of grass behind a log about 20 feet east of the back door. Made from solid maple, the heavy club was nearly three inches wide and two feet in length, cut to have sharp edges. Later, John Porter identified it as a German flail, a tool used for threshing grain. Porter remembered noticing it when the previous tenant had lived there, and he was sure he had seen it in the yard since then. When the sheriff saw dried blood and what looked like human hairs on the club, he speculated that it was a murder weapon.

WHEN MARK returned with Wesley later that morning, people scrutinized the boy. With his slight physique—he stood four feet, seven inches tall and weighed about 70 pounds—Wesley appeared younger than his eleven years, physically immature, with the soft face of a child. It was difficult to imagine the boy, alone in the dark house, discovering the disfigured and bloody bodies of his father and stepmother, a sight that had sickened and horrified grown men. Remarkably, Wesley didn't look stricken or even tearful, and he kept to himself in the yard.

Several men approached Wesley to offer their sympathies and to ask him what he knew. Wesley was unemotional as he repeated the story that he had told his brother: he was sleeping in the barn when someone killed his parents. He hadn't heard any noises except a gunshot and then a scream coming from the house. Wesley didn't volunteer more details until someone asked him about the dog, noting that it wasn't around. Wesley couldn't say where the dog was now; it often ran off during the day, coming back at night for food. He had seen it the night before, lying quietly in its usual place near the back door. The men left Wesley alone then, but they wondered about the dog; surely it would have barked if a stranger had entered the house, and the noise would have alerted Wesley before the gun went off.

Perhaps, the neighbors said to each other, the boy was still in a state of shock that might account for his odd manner. Others noted that no one had found bedclothes in the hay, although Wesley would have slept next to the animals in the barn. If he were in the barn, would he even have heard a gunshot coming from the bedroom? George Fairfield suggested a test. He stood in the barn while Deputy Place stood inside the house and fired a single shot through the open window with a 32-caliber revolver. According to Fairfield, the noise could be heard in the barn and sounded like a firecracker.

Who would have wanted to kill John and Hattie Elkins? No one knew of anyone who bore a grudge against John Elkins; he still owed money on the sawmill, but he hadn't missed a payment. If nothing had been taken from the house, robbery didn't appear to be the motive. The discovery of the club added to the mystery. Would a stranger have found his weapon in the yard, and then, after using it in the attacks, left it there instead of taking it away?

People didn't believe that Wesley, young as he was, could have committed the crime. Maybe he was making up a story to protect another person.

Late Wednesday afternoon, the county coroner, J. W. Cain, arrived with two local physicians, F. J. Kriebs and Lewis Blanchard. Cain selected three men, all residents of Elk Township, to serve as the inquest jury: George Masters, Kelly Rulon, and H. F. Beyer. They were charged with questioning witnesses and making an initial determination about the crime. Fairfield, the newspaper man, was asked to take notes and serve as the official recorder.

Before assembling in the larger room, the men filed into the bedroom to view the murder victims. Temperatures had soared over 100 degrees, and the air inside was stifling. The bodies had stiffened, but they were just as the Porters had found them. John Elkins was reclining on his side, with his head on the pillow, and Hattie was lying across his lower half, with her eyes staring at the ceiling. The men took note of the blood, now turned nearly black, which had pooled on the floor and splattered the walls.

When the jurors left, the doctors had their turns. They took their time examining the bodies, carefully noting and cataloging the extensive injuries suffered by the victims of the brutal attack.

2.

LESS THAN TWENTY-FOUR HOURS after his father and step-mother were murdered, Wesley Elkins entered the house to answer questions from the inquest jury. He was the first of nearly a dozen people to be interrogated.

As the young boy faced the three men, he was pale and composed. He was still barefoot and wearing the same overalls and shirt he had worn that morning, and the jurors could see that both were spotted with blood. At the coroner's instruction, Wesley raised his hand and swore to tell the truth. Then, in a tone one juror described as "remarkably cool," Wesley told his story of the previous night. The boy mostly kept his head down, staring at the floor, as he spoke. When he did look up, the jurors noticed that one eye had a visible twitch.

Wesley said that he had eaten supper with his parents, and then had gone to bed in the barn around 8 P.M. His father had told him to sleep there, and he didn't mind; it was cooler than inside the house.

Sometime after dark, he said, he was awakened by a gunshot followed by a woman's scream. He thought it was his stepmother, and she sounded like she was hurt. He was sure the shot had come from the house, but he didn't hear anything else after that: no dog barking or footsteps. He was scared, and so he waited a while—maybe thirty minutes—before he dared to leave the barn.

When he finally ventured outside, he entered the house from the back. That door was partly ajar, and he called out to his parents. No one responded, and then he heard his sister, Nellie, "crying bad, hard as it could." He found her in his parents' bedroom, lying at the top of the bed next to the still forms of his father and stepmother. He thought right away that they were dead, and he was careful not to touch them as he reached for the baby. He carried her into the other bedroom, lit the lamp, and changed her out of her bloody clothes. When he left the house, he noticed that the clock said 3:30 A.M. When the sun started to rise, he hitched the horse to the buggy and took his sister with him to fetch his older brother, Mark.

Wesley told the jurors that nothing peculiar had happened the evening before; his father had gone shooting and came back with a squirrel that he had given the dog to eat. Wesley hadn't heard his parents quarrelling as he left the house. He had been sleeping in the barn for several nights, and he always slept directly on the hay. When one of the jurors produced the suspected murder weapons, Wesley said that he had never seen the club before. He did recognize his father's rifle. His father always hung it on the wall in the second bedroom after using it, and Wesley had seen it hanging there while he changed the baby's clothes. His father had taught him how to use it. Wesley demonstrated by picking up the rifle and aiming it at the wall.

One man asked Wesley to step into the bedroom and measure his feet against the tracks on the floor. Wesley didn't hesitate; he walked to the bed where the dead bodies still lay and stepped directly on one of the bloody prints. His foot, which was smaller than a man's, corresponded exactly. Finally, Wesley was asked if he had any idea who might have murdered his parents. Wesley responded, "I don't have any idea as to who had been in the house and don't suspect anyone."

When the two doctors were ready with their report, the jurors dismissed Wesley and told him to wait outside. The men came in together to report their findings and offer their reconstruction of the murders. They believed that John Elkins had been shot first, and it was possible that the assailant was standing outside the window when he pulled the trigger. The bullet had entered Elkins' left eye socket and exited near the top of his head; the doctors had discovered the bullet buried in his feather pillow. Although he had almost certainly died from the gunshot, John Elkins had also been beaten around the face.

Hattie was not killed immediately. The position of her body suggested that she must have heard the shot, risen from the bed, and turned to face her husband, with her back to the door. If the attacker had been outside, he must have come in the house, then entered the bedroom and assaulted Hattie. He had struck Hattie from behind with a blunt heavy object, and the blow was powerful enough to break the occipital bone at the base of her skull. She had fallen back on the bed, face up, partially covering her husband. Although the initial blow would have knocked her senseless, the murderer had come close to the bed and continued to beat her. The front of her skull had been crushed by multiple blows to her forehead, and her cheekbone and jaw were fractured; both her legs were badly bruised above and below the knees.

Dr. Kriebs and Dr. Blanchard confirmed what the men on the jury already suspected. The doctors were sure that Elkins had been shot with his own rifle. The bullet that killed him fit that gun and was the same type stored in his ammunition box. Furthermore, they had no doubt that the victims had been attacked with the heavy wooden club found in the yard; its dimensions exactly fit the contours of Hattie's injuries.

With the identification of the murder weapons, the jury could limit the pool of suspects. There seemed little doubt that the killer had been familiar with the place. He knew where John Elkins kept his rifle and the killer took the time to put it back in its place after the attack. He must have seen the club in the yard before he killed his victims, and then, when he was sure that the couple was dead, he had tried to hide it there.

Before the inquest began, neighbors had wondered about Mark Elkins, John's oldest son. He was a strong young man, and they knew that he had quarreled with his father, who disapproved of Mark playing cards with friends in the evenings. Mark had made no secret of his dislike for Hattie, and it seemed likely that there were other conflicts. Several years earlier, Mark had told his friends that he could not live with John and Hattie anymore. He had moved away, renting a room nearby at the Woodall farmhouse, though he often came to see the family to discuss business at the sawmill with his father and to visit with Wesley.

If the jurors suspected Mark, their doubts were soon dispelled. Mark had an alibi that was confirmed by others. Mark repeated the story he had told to neighbors: he had spent the entire previous evening and night in his room at the Woodall farm, waking only when Wesley shouted from the porch. Mr. Woodall reported that he was sure Mark was telling the truth. He and Mark had sat on his porch talking that evening until long after dark. They went inside together, and he saw Mark go into his bedroom. Mr. Woodall awoke when he heard Wesley, and he had joined Mark on the porch to talk to the boy. He had seen for himself that Mark was shocked and upset by the news, and that Mark had rushed immediately to go to his father's house.

One juror asked if Woodall was sure that Mark had been in the house all night.

Woodall answered with certainty. Mark's room didn't have a door to the outside, and Woodall would have heard if the front door had opened. According to Woodall, Mark "couldn't get out of the room without my knowing it."

The jurors followed up with another boarder at Woodall's home—Alice Cooper, an eighteen-year-old woman—who testified to the same effect. Her room was also close to Mark's, and she knew she would have woken if he had left the house. Like Mr. Woodall, she had not been disturbed until she heard Wesley shouting from the porch.

The men on the jury had more questions for Mark. Asked about his parents, Mark didn't acknowledge any tensions or conflicts in the past: "I never had any quarrel with father, and not to amount to anything with mother." He said he had visited his parents a few days earlier and talked with his brother. Wesley hadn't told him that he was sleeping in the barn, and he hadn't confided that he was unhappy. Mark believed that Wesley "got along well" with his parents.

Did Mark suspect anyone of committing the crime? Mark had no one to suggest: "I don't know of anyone who has anything against father, and I don't know of anything which would aid in finding the murderer." One juror asked, "Do you know of any person you would like sworn?" Mark responded, "No, I believe not."

Might Wesley be guilty? Mark responded to the question: "I never saw [Wesley] shoot the gun. . . . I do not think he could have shot father."

Once Mark was eliminated as a suspect, the jurors focused again on Wesley. The boy knew where his father kept his rifle, and he had admitted being on the property that night. No evidence of an intruder had been found. Wesley had the means and the opportunity to commit the crime, but would he have been strong enough to wield the club? And what could have made him angry enough to commit such a violent crime?

Other witnesses had mentioned that Wesley had run away from home a few weeks before the murder, and the jurors wanted to know more about that. Alfred Heath, a farmer who lived on the outskirts of Elk Township, offered some information. Wesley had arrived unexpectedly at his home around 2 P.M. one afternoon. Hiram Cooper, the owner of a neighboring farm, had driven Wesley there, although Cooper didn't stay to talk to Heath. Wesley had not said much to Heath except that he wanted to get away from his father. Although his birth mother was dead, Wesley wished to return to Waterloo where he had lived with her. Heath would not agree to take him, but Wesley refused to leave and sat quietly in the house for eight hours, until long after dark. It was near

10 P.M. when John Elkins, tipped off by a neighbor about his son's whereabouts, arrived at Heath's house and demanded that Wesley come home with him.

The jurors called Wesley back in the room. They wanted to know more about his and Mark's relationship with their father. Wesley told them that John Elkins was "quick tempered, he got mad quick, and he would swear when he got mad." He knew that his father and Mark had clashed over Mark's gambling, but, Wesley said, Elkins was "a good father to his boys," and he treated them well.

Had Wesley ever been punished or mistreated at home? Wesley replied, "Father whipped me pretty hard last winter. . . . Never whipped me since."

If he got along so well at home, why had he tried to run away? Wesley admitted that he had left home, but he blamed Hiram Cooper for that. Cooper and his father didn't get along, and Cooper had urged him to leave. Wesley said that Cooper tried to coax him away several times before, but Wesley hadn't gone until this last time. He knew his father would be angry if he found out.

Other testimony had suggested to the jurors that the Coopers were concerned about Wesley. According to Mark, Alice Cooper, Hiram Cooper's daughter, had approached him at some point before the run-away attempt. She said that she and her father believed Wesley was being mistreated and abused at home. She was afraid for the boy's safety and appealed to Mark to get him away from John and Hattie. The Cooper family, she said, would take care of the young boy, feeding and clothing him until he was old enough to fend for himself. Mark remembered the conversation with Alice, though he didn't believe her. He hadn't taken her advice, and Wesley stayed where he was.

When Cooper and his daughter were questioned, they both denied that they had attempted to intervene in John Elkins' private affairs. Neither one would admit that they had worried about Wesley. Alice denied the conversation with Mark, and Cooper told a story that was different from Wesley's. Yes, Cooper had given the boy a ride, but he had never encouraged Wesley to leave home. Wesley had been at the side of the road when Cooper was driving by, and he had asked Cooper to take him away. Wesley had also begged him not to reveal his whereabouts to his father, and Cooper had agreed to keep the secret. As he told the inquest jury, he regretted that. Elkins was angry when he found out that Cooper had played a role in Wesley's run-away attempt, and the two men exchanged heated words. Cooper later apologized, and he testified that he believed he and Elkins were on good terms after that.

Other witnesses agreed that Wesley had tried to run away from home. To the jury, that suggested that he was unhappy, but it was hardly sufficient proof as a motive for murder.

One of the jurors, Mr. Beyer, wanted to question Wesley again. He had suspected from the beginning that Wesley was not telling the truth. He was particularly bothered by Wesley's manner, which seemed strange for a child who had just been orphaned; he was too calm, without even a show of grief. Most significant to Beyer, though, was Wesley's statement to his brother about exactly how his parents had been killed. There couldn't have been much light in the room, and Wesley said he didn't touch the bodies, so how could he have known that his father and Hattie were dead?

When Wesley was called a third time, Beyer challenged him on several points. Cooper had denied that he had tried to urge Wesley to leave home. Was Wesley telling the truth about that? Wesley admitted that he had lied, saying now that he had left because he had a bad headache and not because anyone had told him to leave.

If he were lying then, Beyer asked, how could the men trust that he was telling the truth about other aspects of his story? How could Wesley have known what had happened to his parents when he entered the bedroom? At 3:30 A.M., wasn't it completely dark? It was mostly dark, Wesley said, but there was moonlight coming in the bottom of window. And yet, Beyer said, it had been days since the moon had been full, and the curtains were pulled down when the bodies were found the next day. He could see a bit, Wesley said, and he must have lit the lamp in that room and not in the other room when he changed the baby. But then why were the matches found in the second bedroom? Wesley had no answer to that. Beyer continued: Even if there were some light in the room, how could Wesley have known right away that they were dead? If he hadn't touched the bodies, how could he tell exactly how they had been killed, that his father had been shot and his stepmother beaten to death? Wesley responded that he could see blood dripping on the floor, and he bent down close enough to see the hole in his father's head.

Although Beyer wasn't satisfied, it was nearly evening, and Coroner Cain thought they had heard enough. Cain brought the proceeding to a close and asked the three jurors to decide on a verdict. Beyer argued that Wesley's story was riddled with inconsistencies and that Wesley should be named in their decision and then arrested. Masters and Rulon were not so sure, and eventually they convinced Beyer to sign a verdict addressing only the manner of deaths: John Elkins had died from a gunshot wound and a blow to his head and Hattie Elkins from beatings with a blunt instrument, with the fatal injuries in both cases inflicted "by a person or persons unknown to the jury."

When the jury was dismissed, Beyer took Sheriff Kann aside and urged him to take Wesley into custody. George Muegge, a neighbor who had been at the house, also spoke to the sheriff, advising Kann not to leave without taking the boy. Kann wasn't convinced by either man. He explained that he did not have enough evidence to link Wesley to the crime. Until then, Kann said, the boy was free to go.

It was dark by the time Wesley was taken away in a buggy driven by his uncle, Alfred Tubbs. Tubbs and his wife, Melissa, had agreed to take Wesley to their home in the nearby township of Honey Creek. Melissa Tubbs, the sister of John Elkins, refused to believe a young boy like Wesley was capable of murder.

On Wednesday evening, as darkness descended and the air cooled, most of the people still in the Elkins yard returned to their farms. Mark Elkins left for his rented room. Inside the house, the two corpses, now stiff with rigor mortis, were carried to the larger room. Several of the neighbor women stayed to prepare the body of Hattie Elkins for burial. A neighbor named C. W. Wooldridge promised the sheriff that he would take care of the body of John Elkins and watch over the house through the night.

After the others left, Wooldridge carried the bed frame and bloody bedclothes into the yard. He lit the pile on fire and watched it burn to ashes.

3.

JOHN AND HATTIE ELKINS had both been raised in Clayton County, and they were well-known to residents there. They had been married for seven years when they were killed. John, who had been married twice before, was twenty years older than Hattie. At the time of their marriage, he was thirty-six, and she was sixteen.

As a teenager, John had served in the Union Army and worked as a farmhand until he purchased the sawmill. His first wife, Phoebe, had died young, leaving him with two children. By 1889, they were both adults. At the time of the murders, Mark, twenty-one years old, lived close to his father; Cora, nineteen, resided with her husband and two children in Minnesota. Eleven-year-old Wesley was John's son by his second wife, Matilda Blackwell. Stories about that unfortunate marriage, ending in scandal and divorce, had long circulated among the neighbors.

Matilda Blackwell was born and raised in Keokuk, Iowa, nearly 200 miles south of Elkader, and she wasn't known by Clayton County residents when she wed John Elkins sometime in the mid-1870s. Their marriage was stormy from the start. Matilda was rumored to be an immoral and unstable woman who was solely to blame for their marital troubles. It was alleged that she had taken a lover while she was married to John and pregnant with his child, and then, with the baby in her womb, she had plotted to kill her husband either with poison or a gun. Ultimately, she didn't go through with either plan. Instead, she deserted Elkins and moved to Waterloo where, according to the gossip in Clayton County, she lived in shame with her lover. Although divorce was uncommon at the time, John and Matilda dissolved their marriage soon after Matilda left.

The historical record tells a somewhat different story. We know that shortly after giving birth to John's child in Clayton County, Matilda had moved away, leaving the infant—named John Wesley—with his father. Wesley spent his earliest years with his father, who lived in rented rooms and worked on a neighbor's farm. Most likely Wesley was cared for by his older half-sister, Cora.

John Elkins didn't keep his son for long. In 1882, when he married young Hattie Outcalt, a neighbor's daughter, he sent four-year-old Wesley to live with his birth mother in Waterloo, about seventy miles southwest of Elkader. By then, Matilda had a new family. After divorcing John Elkins, she married William Dowden, a widower with two children: a son named Will, several years older than Wesley, and a daughter named Georgianna, four years old, the same age as Wesley. Matilda and William had one more child after Wesley arrived: a son, Elmer, who was born blind.

Wesley spent three years in Waterloo with his mother, and he grew close to the Dowden family. But his life was uprooted once again when he was seven years old. Matilda died shortly after Elmer's birth, and William, left alone with four young children, decided that Wesley should be returned to his father.

When Wesley arrived unexpectedly back in Clayton County, neighbors speculated that his stepfather must have thrown him out of the house. John and Hattie did not welcome the boy into their home and sent him to live with Hattie's parents, the Outcalts, who had a son about the same age as Wesley. The two boys went to school together for two years, but then Hattie's mother refused to keep him longer. She told her daughter that the boy was bad-tempered and quarrelsome, and she insisted that John and Hattie take him back. By the time he was nine, Wesley had been forced to move five times.

John Elkins didn't allow Wesley to continue at school. A few years earlier, he had purchased a sawmill where he put Wesley to work. Neighbors saw Wesley tending the fire there, and they wondered why Elkins would have his young child do such an arduous job. Elkins bragged to neighbors that he was saving the cost of hiring another person.

In the evenings, Wesley was supervised by Hattie. She was known to be strict, and people understood that she disliked and resented her stepson. Visitors to the house remembered that, as soon as Wesley returned to the house, she demanded that he do physical chores outside: milking the cows, feeding the animals, carrying water from the pump to the house. When he completed those tasks, Hattie charged him with taking care of the baby, Nellie, who had been born in the seventh year of John and Hattie's marriage.

Once Wesley stopped going to school, he was isolated from others his age, and few people knew much about him. His teachers, however, remembered him as an eager student. He was, they reported, reserved and shy, and always quick to understand the lessons. Despite the reports from Hattie's mother, neither his teachers nor his schoolmates had thought of him as a troublemaker. Outside of class, Wesley kept to himself and didn't engage in games or rough play with the other boys.

The inquest jury had heard from Mark that the Coopers believed Wesley was abused by his father and stepmother. The jurors asked questions about Wesley's attempt to run away, but they didn't ask the witnesses much about Wesley's home life. In later years, other neighbors would disclose they also thought that Wesley was badly mistreated at home. When he was older, Wesley would admit that he had been physically punished many times and often went to bed bruised and sore from the beatings.

Even if other people had their suspicions about Wesley's home life, few of them would have dared to intervene or to question how parents chose to discipline their children. The inquest jury apparently shared the community's view that it wasn't their concern.

More than a decade later, a minister who worked in the locality would describe what he had known about Wesley in the years before the murders.

"He was a sadly neglected child . . . who was threatened and beaten and cursed at home by his parents, especially by his father. . . . Surely his life as a child had not a ray of light or joy. His little life was crushed, and every legitimate aspiration was broken down by hard and cruel home treatment."

4.

CLAYTON COUNTY, where John and Hattie Elkins were murdered, lies in the northeast corner of Iowa. Covering nearly 800 square miles, it is the fifth largest county in the state. The Mississippi River flows along its eastern borders, where steep cliffs rise nearly 600 feet above the water. Turkey River, one of the Mississippi's tributaries, curves through the middle of the county, and numerous other waterways, including Bear Creek near the Elkins rented house, crisscross the land. Residents took pride in the county's abundant waterpower, thick timber stands, and rich farmland well suited for growing wheat, corn, and oats.

The county was divided into twenty-two townships, with Elk Township—originally named for the animal herds populating its woods and pastures—along the southern border. The area was divided into an uneven checkerboard of farms, some less than twenty acres in size and others more than ten times that large. Many of the pioneer families who staked their claims in the 1840s still owned their farms. The men came together during harvest time and gathered to do business or discuss politics in the small village of Wood Centre, a crossroads with a general store. The women conversed at church and occasional social gatherings at schoolhouses. As in most rural areas, newspapers were essential sources of information. The *Elkader Register* was the county paper with the largest circulation, boasting more than 1,500 readers and offering tidbits about county residents as well as coverage of local and national news.

George Fairfield, the editor of the *Register,* had accompanied Sheriff Kann to the Elkins house the morning after the crime, and he had spent most of that day there. He understood that the bloody double homicide would attract intense attention. Clayton County prided itself on its reputation as peaceable and law-abiding, and it had been nearly ten years since a murder had occurred there. In that case an elderly man was shot while sitting inside his house reading the newspaper. The gunshot had come from outside the house, and the victim died instantaneously. He was a wealthy man, not well-liked and said to be difficult and hard on anyone who owed him money; his death didn't provoke much sympathy among the locals. His brother was accused of the murder, but the case against him was dropped for lack of evidence. A second suspect was arrested and acquitted after a jury trial. Interest faded in the case, although people hadn't forgotten that authorities had failed to solve the crime.

On Thursday morning, the *Cedar Rapids Republican*, a daily newspaper with a much wider circulation than the *Register*, ran a short article on its front page. It covered a single column, most of which was taken up by a bold headline beginning, "THE SLEEP OF DEATH. NIGHT CLOSES IN ON JOHN ELKINS AND WIFE AS THEY LAY DOWN TO THEIR LAST SLEEP." The headline went on to proclaim: "ELKINS FOUND WRITHING IN THE DEATH AGONY WITH A BULLET THROUGH HIS BRAIN," and "HIS YOUNG WIFE ALSO FOUND DEAD ON THE BED WITH HER HEAD MASHED IN," while "A SLEEPING BABE BETWEEN THE MURDERED COUPLE WAS SPARED BY THE MIDNIGHT ASSASSIN." According to the *Republican*, suspicion had already focused on the two sons who held a grudge against their stepmother.

Although Fairfield's newspaper, the *Elkader Register*, reached fewer people, he knew it would be read widely by those who knew the Elkins family. Also he could share more lurid details. He had been at the house and seen the bodies, he had participated in the investigation, and he had attended the inquest.

The *Register*, a weekly paper circulated on Thursday mornings, was printed the day after the crime was discovered. That was for-

tuitous timing for Fairfield. His article covered two full columns
running the length of the front page. The bold headline read:
"HORRIBLE MURDER! JOHN ELKINS AND WIFE, OF ELK TOWN-
SHIP, KILLED IN THEIR HOUSE ON WEDNESDAY MORNING. THE
MOST REVOLTING MURDER IN THE HISTORY OF CLAYTON CO.
NO CLUE AS TO WHO IS GUILTY OF THE CRIME." The article that
followed contained graphic and sensationalistic details.

Under the subheading "At the Scene," Fairfield described the
location of the house. Under "Horrible Sight" and "The Body of
Mrs. Elkins," he reported seeing the victims just hours after the
murders, when the "frightfully mangled bodies" still lay on the
bed. He gave details of John Elkins' wounds: his shattered left eye
where the bullet had entered, and his skull which was "crushed
to jelly" by a blow to his right temple. Fairfield then recreated
how Hattie must have died: she had been awakened by the shot
that killed her husband and "had sprang out on the floor and
had made a struggle for her life but to no avail." She had suffered
blows to her head from the front and the back, shattering her
skull and breaking her jawbone, and she had been beaten up and
down her legs.

Fairfield described his search for the murder weapons: he had
discovered the blood-stained wooden club in the yard, and he had
seen the rifle and the bullet taken from the pillow behind John
Elkins' head. As the recorder for the inquest jury, he could also
summarize the testimony of Wesley and the other witnesses. Fairfield told his readers that the authorities were working hard, but
they had made "no headway in the matter, everything seemingly
being surrounded with a veil of mystery."

One week later, a group of seven prominent county officials—
including the sheriff, the county attorney, the clerk of court, and
the coroner—drafted and signed a letter to the Iowa governor,
William Larrabee. The murders, they wrote, were among the
"most brutal and atrocious" ever committed in Iowa. No one had
been punished for the earlier crime in Clayton County, and so it

was particularly important that the murderer be found. The men proposed a reward be offered for help in solving the case, and Governor Larrabee agreed, declaring that $500 would be paid "for the arrest and delivery to the proper authorities of the person or persons" guilty of the murder of John Elkins and Hattie Elkins. In the *Register,* Fairfield stressed that if the crime could not be solved, it would be "a shadow of shame upon our county."

THE MURDERS created intense anxiety and excitement in Clayton County. Although people had initially suspected that Mark Elkins was involved, they now knew he had an alibi. Since there was no evidence of an intruder, attention focused on Wesley.

With his childish appearance and reserved manner, he was certainly an unlikely suspect. As one neighbor put it, "he was too small and good a boy to be guilty of such a crime." A friend of Mark's spoke up for Wesley, describing him as "precocious, extremely industrious, quiet and retiring in disposition." Another expressed the feelings of many, that his youth made it impossible to imagine he could be guilty. If he were involved, he could not have acted alone; he must have had an accomplice or help from someone older.

Wesley continued to repeat his story, but the circumstantial evidence pointed to him. He had the opportunity to commit the crime, and he had both weapons close at hand. His cool manner also seemed to implicate him. Should he not have been horrified and grief-stricken when he told John Porter that he found his parents had been killed?

Even those who suspected Wesley were mystified by the crime. The idea that a child, as normal looking as one's own, could commit such violence seemed incomprehensible and too horrible to believe, at least, that is, until the rumors about his mother, Matilda, began once again to circulate through the community. The whispered stories were repeated from neighbor to neighbor, painting an indelible picture of her, an image that would influence people's views about Wesley then and in the years to come. Many came to believe that it was no longer important to try to understand Wesley's motive behind the crime. It was far easier to believe that he was immoral and depraved from the day he was born; had inherited his mother's murderous disposition, making him capable of killing his father and stepmother; and had done so without reason or remorse. As a reporter would later say, many Clayton County residents were convinced that Wesley Elkins was "born with the brand of Cain on his brow."

Several people spoke directly to Sheriff Kann, urging him to take Wesley into custody. H. F. Beyer, a member of the inquest jury, continued to argue for Wesley's arrest. As the investigation progressed with no reports of clues, Robert Quigley, the Clayton County prosecutor, also approached Kann. Quigley identified Wesley as the most important witness, and he wanted to be sure the boy was available for more questioning. The prosecutor, who had learned that Wesley had a sister in Minnesota, was afraid that Wesley would leave his uncle's house to go there. Privately, Quigley believed the rumors about Wesley's mother, and that her son had inherited a criminal gene from her. Quigley was convinced that Wesley was guilty and would not hesitate to kill again.

Sheriff Kann, still in his first year in office, was not persuaded by the suspicions of the community. He knew that prosecutions often failed because of insufficient evidence, and he was determined to avoid that result. The investigation was still ongoing, and there was no end in sight. Frustrated by the lack of progress in the investigation, the sheriff contacted the famed Pinkerton Agency in Chicago and asked to hire a detective.

As it turned out, the Pinkerton Agency's help would not be necessary to solve the case.

JOHN AND HATTIE ELKINS were buried on Thursday, July 18, less than forty-eight hours after they had been murdered. Wesley attended the service at Edgewood Cemetery with his aunt and uncle, Alfred and Melissa Tubbs. The *Elkader Register* reported the fact of the burial but offered no details about Wesley's demeanor or actions. After the burial, Wesley returned to Honey Creek with his aunt and uncle.

As their suspicions of Wesley mounted, people in the community expected that he would remain secluded and avoid attention, and so it was a surprise when he came to town with his uncle on Friday. It was another hot day, with temperatures reaching 98 degrees. News of Wesley's appearance spread quickly, and as Wesley and his uncle came into the town center and dismounted their horse buggy, a crowd of men gathered around the boy. For many it was the first time they had seen Wesley in person. One man stepped forward and lifted him off the ground, as if to ascertain his weight.

On Sunday, Sheriff Kann drove to Honey Creek to talk to Wesley and his aunt and uncle. Kann explained that he hoped an outside detective would arrive early in the week, and it was essential that Wesley be available for an interview. He suggested that Wesley come to live with him and his family in Elkader for a few days, although he stressed that Wesley was not under arrest, and he was not obligated to agree. Wesley replied that he was quite willing to stay with Sheriff Kann, and the Tubbs had no objection to the plan.

When they arrived at Kann's residence in Elkader, the sheriff advised Wesley to stay in a back bedroom and away from the windows if he saw people outside. Lynching was uncommon in Iowa in the late 1800s, but Kann was responsible for Wesley's safety, and he was aware of the possibility. In 1883, just sixty miles west of Elkader, the Barber boys, accused of being horse thieves and murderers, had been lynched by an angry mob. Attempted lynchings had been thwarted elsewhere in Iowa in the late 1880s. Recognizing the rising tide of emotion in Clayton County, and by nature a cautious man, Kann did not want Wesley Elkins to suffer the same fate. The sheriff also let Wesley know that, at least in the eyes of the public, he was still a prime suspect.

Three days later the *Dubuque Daily Times* printed a front-page article appearing under the headline "A YOUNG FIEND" and stating that Wesley Elkins had been arrested for the murder of his parents. Although that wasn't true, the story reflected the growing belief that Wesley had committed the crime on his own. The article noted the boy's behavior, claiming that he had yet "to shed a tear, flinch, or show the least emotion over the affair."

JAMES CORLETT, a prominent lawyer in Elkport and a friend of the sheriff's, had taken a special interest in the case. As an elected official—Corlett served as clerk of court—he had signed the letter to Governor Larrabee requesting the reward for information about the Elkins case.

Corlett had graduated from the Iowa College of Law ten years earlier, and he was well-versed in criminal law. An ambitious man, he planned to run for county attorney and was eager to get his name known by the public. He was also of the firm belief that Wesley Elkins had committed the crime.

Sheriff Kann gave Corlett permission to visit Wesley, and Corlett took the opportunity to interrogate him. He visited the boy in the afternoons and took him out for buggy rides. When they were alone, Corlett questioned Wesley, asking him to repeat his story. As Corlett said later, he grew increasingly suspicious when Wesley used nearly the same words every time, as if he had memorized what he had decided to say. Although Corlett warned the boy that his lies would be uncovered, Wesley did not change his version. When Sheriff Kann advised Corlett that he planned to return Wesley to his uncle's home, Corlett asked for one more opportunity to find out if Wesley was telling the truth.

On Thursday, July 25, Corlett arrived at the sheriff's house in a two-horse buggy, asking if he could take Wesley to a baseball game in McGregor, twenty miles away. Sheriff Kann gave his permission, and Wesley had little choice but to agree. Kann still believed in Wesley's innocence, so he was surprised when Corlett told him privately that he should be prepared to arrest Wesley later that day.

Alone with Wesley in the buggy, Corlett described to Wesley exactly how the state punished murderers who lied and were later found to be guilty. Corlett had first-hand knowledge of how a man died on the gallows, and he offered a graphic description. Just eighteen months earlier, in his capacity as clerk of court, Corlett had witnessed an execution in Fayette County, close to the road where he and Wesley were traveling. Twenty-year-old Henry Schmidt had been convicted of killing an elderly couple, and although he claimed to be innocent, he was sentenced to death. Corlett heard the young man's last words, denying responsibility for the crime. He told Wesley that he watched as Schmidt climbed the steps to the gallows where the executioner fit the noose around his neck and pulled a black cap over his head, covering his face. When the trapdoor was released, Schmidt fell out of sight and died.

Corlett hoped to frighten Wesley into confessing, and he succeeded. Before they reached McGregor, Wesley admitted that he had been lying all along, and that he had killed his father and stepmother.

What exactly did Wesley say to Corlett? We don't know. All we have is Corlett's account of what happened. Corlett reported that he guided the buggy to a stop and took out a pen and paper so he could record what happened next. He instructed Wesley to tell the truth and warned him that he could be put to death if he continued to lie. Corlett said that Wesley remained impassive as he confessed to the murders, showing no signs of fear. He didn't break down or cry. According to Corlett, Wesley stated that he had acted on his own and volunteered that he was sorry for what he had done and for all his lies. Corlett quickly wrote down that

Wesley admitted that he was the murderer, and he had the boy sign his name at the bottom of the page.

Corlett wanted some assurance that Wesley would not change his story. He drove on to McGregor to the home of L. O. Hatch and asked him to listen to the boy's statement. The elderly judge took Wesley into a private room and advised him that he wasn't obliged to say anything against himself.

At the Grand Jury hearing several months later, Hatch testified that Wesley, speaking in a voice that was "perfectly cool and self-possessed," had confessed to the murders to him, as well as to Corlett. We cannot, however, be sure exactly what Wesley told the judge. By the time Hatch testified to the Grand Jury in October, he had certainly read the statement written by Corlett that was widely publicized by the newspapers. Given the similarity of the language, the chronology, and the details, it seems almost certain that Hatch was relying in his testimony on Corlett's statement as the authoritative version of Wesley's story. When Judge Hatch finished relating that story to the Grand Jury, he added a few details about the end of his conversation with Wesley:

> "I then asked why he killed his father and mother. He answered, 'Because I was mad at them. . . . I wanted to go away from home and do for myself and they wouldn't let me, and I ran away and my father came and brought me back and said if I ran away again he would whip me.' I asked if his father had been in the habit of whipping him, and he answered that he had whipped him once last winter, but he said his father was not to blame, that he deserved it. I asked him if he whipped him very hard at that time. He said, 'Yes, pretty hard.'"

> "I said, 'Wesley, why didn't you run away then after you had killed them?' Wesley answered, 'I thought if I did then everybody would think that I did it.'"

> "I then asked why he didn't kill the baby, and he answered, 'I liked the baby and didn't want to kill it.'"

AS SOON AS Judge Hatch ended his meeting with Wesley, Corlett drove the boy back to Elkader. Leaving Wesley with the sheriff, Corlett went directly to the courthouse. He filed a formal complaint charging Wesley Elkins with murder in the first degree, and Judge Isaac Matthews issued an arrest warrant. The warrant was delivered to Sheriff Kann, who officially arrested Wesley and escorted him to the courthouse.

W. E. Odell, a local attorney, was summoned and appointed to represent Wesley. The lawyer took Wesley to stand in front of Judge Matthews, who read the complaint aloud and asked for Wesley's response. According to the formal document later signed by Judge Matthews, Wesley's attorney pled not guilty on behalf of his client and, also on behalf of his client, waived any further examination by the judge.

Judge Matthews ordered that Wesley Elkins be taken into custody, to be held without bond, and to appear at the next term of the District Court. With his thin wrists locked in metal handcuffs, Wesley was then led the short distance to the county jail where he would spend the next six months of his life.

Shortly after Wesley was arrested, Corlett wrote to the governor and claimed the $500 reward for finding and delivering to the authorities the person who killed John and Hattie Elkins. Corlett was not the only person who thought he was entitled to the reward. Two other men would also file statements with the governor's office claiming the reward: H. F. Beyer, the inquest juror, and George Muegge, the local man who had urged the sheriff to arrest Wesley the day the bodies were discovered.

5.

THE NEWS OF Wesley's confession circulated swiftly among residents of Clayton County. Corlett was quick to release a lengthy statement to the newspapers that, he claimed, contained the words spoken by Wesley. Corlett later admitted to the Grand Jury that he did not report Wesley's exact words. After Wesley was taken into custody, Corlett had rewritten the confession under the boy's name to represent the substance of what he had said.

There was no one version of the confession, and statements with minor discrepancies were printed in various newspapers. In one, for example, Wesley purportedly explained that he committed the crime because he was sick of doing chores. According to others, he said that he didn't want to take care of the baby, that he wanted to be "free," or, as the one reported in the *Elkader Register,* that he wanted to "be at liberty to do for myself." All the published accounts provided details to show that Wesley had premediated the crime and intended to kill his parents.

The following statement was the one that appeared under the name of John Wesley Elkins in the *Elkader Register:*

I had wanted to leave home and be at liberty to do for myself for a long time. I once ran away but father brought me home. Two or three days before the 16th day of July, I began planning to kill my parents, and when I came in from milking on that night, I went to the old granary and got the club which was found and placed it on a chair in my room. About 3 o'clock in the morning, I got up and went out of doors and looked all around but saw no one. I then went into the bedroom where father and mother slept and

saw they were asleep. I went back to my room and took the rifle
from the wall where father always hung it and went back to their
room and put the muzzle within about two feet of father's face
and fired.

I ran back to my room and threw the gun on my bed and
grabbed the club which was on a chair near the door; ran back to
their door and saw mother had jumped out of bed upon the floor
and was stooped over as if to light a lamp, when I struck her on
the back of the head with the club; she kind of sprawled backward
upon the bed, and I struck her several times more until I was sure
she was dead, and then father kind of groaned and I struck him
once or twice to be sure he was dead.

After I was sure they were dead, I lit the lamp and took it to my
room and then went back and took the baby from their bed, and
took off its bloody clothes and dressed it and quieted it. Then
I started to load the rifle, but after getting the powder into the
gun, I could not find the balls and other things, and thought I
was fooling around there too long, and went to the back door and
knocked the powder out of the gun by the door step and took the
club and threw it out into the weeds. I then went and hitched up
the old horse and took the baby and drove down by Porters and
they stopped me.

One confession published in a different newspaper reported
that Wesley had ended with these words:

When I got down to Porters, I hollered to them, and all the statements I made contrary to these are false and untrue.

I have been sorry a great many times since I done it, and that I
did not tell it at once, and can hardly realize that I had murdered
them. I took no money or property from the house.

PEOPLE IN Clayton County were stunned by the vivid depiction
of the crime. Although they knew the assaults had been brutal,
the moment-to-moment images of how John and Hattie Elkins

had been killed were far more powerful than the medical reports. The objective and detached tone of the account—as if describing commonplace events—was especially chilling. According to the statement, Wesley had proceeded in a cold-blooded and methodical way, choosing the murder weapons and waiting until the victims were defenseless. The confession attributed to him left no doubt that he had acted with malice aforethought.

Wesley Elkins never repudiated the lengthy statement, but it is difficult to believe that those words were spoken by an eleven-year-old child. The description of the crime is chronological and organized, the details are specific, and the phrasing and sentence structure are more sophisticated than one would expect.

It would have been easy for Corlett to reconstruct what he imagined Wesley had done. He knew exactly what had been found as evidence, and, as a trained attorney, Corlett knew the elements that were necessary to support a conviction of first-degree murder: premeditation, intent, and an understanding of the consequences.

Wesley Elkins would never deny that he had killed his parents. In later years, Wesley and others who knew him explained the murders as the impulsive acts of a child who had been severely abused by his parents. After reading the statement published in the newspapers, though, Clayton County residents could not accept that explanation.

The horror triggered by Wesley's confession was mixed with anger. The boy had lied repeatedly to the investigators and to neighbors. Many who had believed him at first and had offered their sympathies now felt manipulated and tricked. They saw Wesley Elkins as evil, cunning, and manipulative.

As the community sought to make sense of the crime, they speculated that the boy might wear the mask of a child, but was an aberration inside, forever cursed with an unnatural disposition inherited from Matilda Blackwell, his depraved mother. After all, they said, Wesley was in her womb when she thought of murdering John Elkins, the very man Wesley now admitted killing. People theorized that Wesley had absorbed her hatred and her desire to commit violent crimes.

Eleven-year-old Wesley Elkins was now publicly branded as a degenerate and a threat to society. In the opinion of one newspaper reporter, the boy was "utterly devoid of all moral sense."

6.

ON AUGUST 23, four weeks after Wesley's arrest, the District Court appointed David Leighty as the administrator of the Elkins estate and set September 21 as the date for a public auction and cash sale of the property of John Elkins. The sale was to commence at 10 A.M. on John Porter's property at the three-room house where John and Hattie Elkins had been murdered. A public announcement listed the property to be sold: "potatoes, corn, sugar cane, oats, hay, one span of mares, cow and calf, wagon, buggy, harnesses, farming utensils, household and kitchen furniture, tools, sewing machine, steer, saw logs, oils, [and] all other personal property of the late John Elkins of Elk Township." John Elkins still owed $900 on the steam sawmill he had operated, and the right, title, and interest in that contract of purchase were also to be put up for sale.

Despite Wesley's confession, his aunt and uncle, Melissa and Alfred Tubbs, continued to believe that Wesley couldn't have committed the crime on his own. Wesley was kept in isolation at the county jail, and his relatives were not allowed to visit him. On October 15, Melissa Tubbs wrote to the outgoing governor of Iowa, William Larrabee, expressing her doubts: "I with many others think the boy did the deed, but that he was persuaded to do it by some other person." She told the governor she believed people were motivated by the reward rather than by finding out the truth, and she was sure she could find out more if she talked to her nephew in private.

A few weeks later, Alfred Tubbs also tried to intervene and gain access to Wesley. He wrote to the newly elected governor, Horace

Boies, asking for "the privilege of talking with Wesley privately. I am sure he will tell us the whole matter just as it is."

There are no records suggesting that these requests were granted.

In October, Robert Quigley, the county prosecutor, convened a Grand Jury that heard from many of the same people who had testified at the coroner's inquest. The testimony focused on the wounds suffered by the victims, the appearance of the rooms, and the evidence that had been discovered. Several people noted Wesley's seeming indifference and odd behavior after the crime. Judge Hatch related his conversation with Wesley, and Corlett read aloud the long confession he claimed Wesley had given him in the buggy that day three months earlier. Wesley's guilt was not in dispute, and it didn't take long for the Grand Jury to indict Wesley for the first-degree murder of his father and stepmother, a crime that required criminal intent.

Over the next decade, Wesley's case would attract attention from the press across the country, from Seattle to New York. One of the first to comment on the legal proceedings was Carl Snyder, a young editor of the *Daily Nonpareil*, a newspaper published in Council Bluffs, Iowa, a city more than 300 miles to the west of Elkader.

Snyder began making his case in mid-October 1889, arguing that Wesley was too young to be treated as an adult under the law. Noting that Wesley, a child, would be imprisoned with adult male convicts, Snyder vigorously condemned the legal process and suggested that sending the boy to a reform school was more appropriate. The goal of the law and the justice system, he asserted, should be for rehabilitation and not for vengeance. Snyder would argue in subsequent editorials that the treatment of Wesley was "barbarous, brutal, a blunder, and a crime."

WESLEY'S COURT DATE was set for January 11, 1890. By then, W. E. Odell, the lawyer who had represented Wesley at his initial court appearance, had decided he could not continue as the defense counsel. He informed the judge that he was too repulsed by the facts of the crime to advocate for the boy. James Crosby, a twenty-two-year-old lawyer also from Clayton County, eventually agreed to take the job, but he was far from the ideal advocate for Wesley. Many years later, Crosby acknowledged that he had believed from the start that there was no viable defense for Wesley.

When Crosby met with Quigley, the two men discussed the sentencing recommendation. Quigley threatened to recommend that Wesley be put to death. As Quigley would repeat in later years, he believed that Wesley deserved to hang for his crime despite his young age. Iowa allowed capital punishment, although Quigley suspected that no judge was likely to send an eleven-year-old boy to be executed. Crosby didn't object when Quigley recommended the second most extreme punishment, sentencing Wesley to life in prison.

Upon visiting Wesley at the county jail, Crosby informed his client that he had to plead guilty to the crime as charged if he wished to avoid a public hanging. When Wesley talked about his conversations with Crosby in later years, he couldn't remember anything about them or about his court appearances, saying that it was all "just a jumble of confusion."

Wesley had no other advocates in the courtroom. He took Crosby's advice and pled guilty to the crime of killing his father, admitting the facts of the confession attributed to him.

ON A COLD January morning in 1890, Wesley was escorted by Sheriff Kann from the Clayton County jail in Elkader to the county courthouse to appear in front of Judge William Hoyt for sentencing. Three other prisoners, all of whom had pled guilty, accompanied Wesley to the courtroom. Wesley waited while the judge disposed of their cases.

C. H. Barrett was sentenced to three and one-half years in the state penitentiary at Anamosa for the crime of stealing a team of horses from Austin's Livery Stable in McGregor. James McGraw received a sentence of four years at Anamosa for burglarizing Hirschfield's Clothing Store in McGregor. William Wadsworth was sentenced to one year at Anamosa for obtaining money under false pretenses.

And then the diminutive Wesley Elkins walked to the front of the courtroom and stood at the defense table next to his lawyer. Wesley recited the words he had been told to say. Although he had been indicted for killing both his father and his stepmother, his plea covered only the murder of his father. The two lawyers in the courtroom knew that would be enough to impose the most extreme penalty possible for a child of his age.

Judge Hoyt asked Wesley a few routine questions to satisfy himself that the boy understood the consequences of his plea. Before imposing the sentence, the judge asked Corlett to read aloud one of the statements that had appeared in the newspapers. Based on that, Judge Hoyt decided that a conviction for first-degree murder was justified. If Wesley had been guilty of a lesser offense, he might have been sent to an institution for juvenile offenders, but Iowa law gave the judge no discretion when a defendant was found guilty of first-degree murder. Judge Hoyt sentenced eleven-year-old Wesley Elkins to life at hard labor at the Anamosa State Penitentiary, a maximum-security institution that housed the state's most dangerous criminals.

When the *Elkader Register* reported that Wesley was convicted of murder and sent to prison for life, the article, likely written by George Fairfield, informed readers that the boy was utterly lacking in emotion or conscience and that he was "undoubtedly the youngest ever convicted of such a crime in the criminal history of the United States." That assertion was not true, but it amplified the feeling in the community that there was something inherently malevolent about Wesley. In fact, although his age could have been a mitigating factor under the law, the community saw his youth as more proof of innate evil, an immutable trait imbedded in him from birth.

This photo of Wesley Elkins was published in Iowa newspapers at the time of the crime. It also graced the cover of a pamphlet distributed to Iowa legislators in 1902. (Courtesy of Steve Wendl and the Anamosa State Penitentiary Prison History website.)

Next to the full text of Wesley's confession, the *Elkader Register* printed a recent photograph of Wesley Elkins. He is visible only to his shoulders, and someone had given him new clothes. He is dressed in a heavy tweed jacket with a polka-dotted scarf tied in a bow and neatly tucked into the jacket collar. His light brown hair is cut short and carefully combed to the side. His features are soft and unlined, his ears are slightly protruding, and his deep-set, dark blue eyes gaze directly ahead into the camera. He looks serious and vulnerable, like a gentle schoolboy younger than his eleven years. Picking up a newspaper, a reader would see the picture first and then read the confession attributed to Wesley, describing in the voice of an adult exactly how he had planned and carried out two horrific murders.

In the years to come, residents of Clayton County would not forget what they took to be the underlying message. The harmless and child-like appearance of Wesley Elkins masked an unnatural and uncontrollable criminal nature.

THE PRISON YEARS
1890–1902

7.

ON JANUARY 14, 1890, Sheriff Kann arrived at Anamosa State Penitentiary with Wesley Elkins.

The penitentiary was a massive and imposing structure designed in the Gothic architectural style, and its fortress-like appearance was forbidding to new prisoners. Nicknamed the "White Palace of the West," it was built entirely out of high-quality dolomite limestone. Heavy iron doors marked the front entrance. Stone walls, six feet thick and more than twenty-two feet high, extended on either side, surrounding the thirteen-acre prison complex behind. Guard towers were strategically placed around the perimeter, and the men on duty were armed with loaded Winchester rifles. A central tower rose sixty feet into the air; the guard manning this station had to be raised and lowered by a pulley. Electric lights on top of a 150-foot smokestack illuminated the yard at night, and the glow of the lights could be seen thirty miles away in Manchester. Inside the structure, derricks and scaffolding had been erected to continue the construction of additions and interior walls.

Sheriff Kann relinquished custody of Wesley to a prison staff member who escorted the boy through the intake process. He was taken to the bathhouse where he was washed and disinfected and to the barbershop where his head was shaved. Then he was ushered to the receiving room, where he was assigned number "1900," which would be used to identify him. Clothes that would be his uniform were adjusted to fit him and stamped with his number. Wesley handed over what he was wearing and changed into those that would mark him as a convict: shirts and pants with horizontal black stripes, a vest to wear under the shirt for warmth, underwear, a coat, a cap, and shoes. He was weighed and interviewed, and the results were recorded by hand under his name in Anamosa's Convict Register.

County From:	Clayton
Crime:	Murder First Degree
Term:	Life
Occupation:	Farmer
Nativity:	Iowa
Social Status:	Single
Mental Culture:	Poor
Religious Education:	None
Habits:	Temperate
Complexion:	Light
Weight:	76 pounds
Height:	4' 7"
Boot Size:	4
Age:	11

MARQUIS BARR was the warden at Anamosa when Wesley arrived in 1890. Barr was forty-six years old and beginning his third two-year term as warden. Although he would step down as warden two years later, Barr would prove to be one of the most significant influences in Wesley's life.

Born in Indiana, Barr grew up near Oskaloosa, in Mahaska County, Iowa. He served as a private with the Union Army in the 47th Iowa Volunteer Infantry during the Civil War, returned to farming after the war, and was elected county sheriff. When the state legislature chose him for the top job at Anamosa, Barr and his family—his pregnant wife, Augusta, and their five children, ranging in age from one to twelve—settled into the comfortable two-story warden's residence. Close enough to the prison so Barr could walk to work, the house was luxurious: more than 3,000 square feet in size, featuring wall hangings and draperies from the finest shops in New York.

Barr had a scholarly look, favoring wire-rimmed glasses and a thick mustache, and he represented a more intellectual and professional breed of prison officials than those in the past. He was interested in prison philosophies, and he had been convinced by new ideas put forth by reformers who believed that prisons should be designed to rehabilitate criminals rather than to punish them. Barr understood that this was a significant transformation in ideas about social control.

Previously, from colonial times and through the first half of the century, crime had been explained as the product of free will; the stated goal of incarceration was to force the prisoner to repent by enforcing strict rules and harsh penalties. Minor infractions often brought physical punishments, such as flogging or stretching, a method that involved attaching the prisoner's arms to ropes hanging from the ceiling.

By the mid-1850s, however, with increasing recidivism, soaring costs to the state, and overcrowded prisons, many had begun to question the effectiveness of these methods. Journalists had drawn attention to the poverty that often prevailed in urban centers, and social scientists focused on external forces as the causes of crime. Reformers were persuaded that prison wardens should aim to improve the character and behavior of those in their charge, enabling them to rejoin and contribute to society. Prisons across the country were experimenting with innovative strategies that offered educational and vocational training, spiritual instruction, and incentives for good conduct.

Warden Barr was convinced that rehabilitative goals were appropriate, and he was grateful to have an institution planned with that in mind.

Anamosa State Penitentiary had been authorized by the Iowa legislature in 1872, chosen in large part because of its location close to a limestone quarry. While the state saved money by using the limestone to build the prison and to sell, the quarry also provided an important opportunity for prisoners to learn skills to help them in the outside world. Those who could be trusted were trained in extracting the heavy stone and worked at the quarry. Others were taught how to cut and shape the stone and construct the buildings where they would serve their time. The men were to be rewarded for their physical exertions: the state legislature had endorsed reduction of sentences for good behavior, which included working more than the required minimum.

Citizens of Anamosa were pleased that their town was selected as the site for the penitentiary, welcoming the new jobs that it would offer. Through the early months of 1873, they watched as hired men erected a small stone building with temporary wooden cells. It was surrounded by a sixteen-foot-high wooden stockade enclosing an area of eleven acres. The entrance to the stockade was fortified with thick iron doors.

In May 1873, a crowd of townspeople was on hand as the prison's first warden, Martin Heisey, stood outside the stockade to greet twenty convicts transferred from Fort Madison. The men were shackled together in pairs and walked two-by-two through the heavy doors and disappeared behind the walls. The *Anamosa Eureka* reported that these men were chosen based on their reliability and physical strength. They were young—the average age was twenty-four—and most had committed nonviolent crimes. Larceny and robbery, which both carried sentences of four years or less, were most common.

Prisoner number "1" in the Convict Register was John Barlow. A twenty-two-year-old carpenter from Clinton County, Barlow was one of only three married men, and he had already served half of his two-year sentence for larceny. According to prison records, he was five-foot, six-inches tall and weighed 130 pounds. The thumb on his left hand was missing, and his right arm sported a tattoo of a woman dancing with a garland over her head.

The *Eureka* was upbeat, noting that the new prisoners "with a few exceptions, wore countenances not by any means altogether vicious or dejected." The reporter added that "they may well have committed less crime against humanity and caused less misery than some who will look coldly upon them in their prison garb." The townspeople took a certain proprietary interest in "our prisoners," as they were called by the local newspaper. Most citizens believed that convicts could be led on a path toward improvement, and members of church congregations urged their ministers to visit the men behind bars. The Ladies' Library Association donated books and reading materials. In August 1873, just a few months after the penitentiary opened its doors, members of the Sabbath School obtained permission to sponsor a picnic in the main prison yard. They shook hands with the convicts, who had been freed from restraints. The guards put away their weapons and watched the group play croquet and other games. Food was provided at tables especially set up for the event, and at the end of the meal, male guests and prisoners mingled and smoked cigars.

When Wesley arrived in 1890, the population of Anamosa numbered 270 men, including eleven lifers. Seventeen women, many convicted of prostitution, were housed in a separate structure. Many of the permanent administration buildings and cellhouses had been completed, and others—including new facilities for the Female and the Insane Departments—were still underway.

All prisoners had daily responsibilities contributing to the upkeep and sustenance of the prison. The women spent their days sewing, mending, and washing clothes, and they ate their meals separately. Some men traveled to the quarry, while most stayed inside the complex. They worked on construction crews and served the prison population by cooking, cleaning, tending the large prison garden, and taking care of other needs of those at Anamosa.

By 1890, the penitentiary was on its way to becoming a model for prisons around the country. It was nearly self-sustaining, supplying its own produce, meat, and milk. Convicts were engaged in productive work and often learned new and specialized skills. Warden Barr, like other progressive wardens, had also designed programs to encourage psychological and spiritual growth.

The penitentiary had a full-time chaplain, and on Sunday mornings after breakfast, prisoners could choose to attend church services. Women sat upstairs in the east balcony, and the men congregated in the long wooden pews on the main floor. The chapel was spacious with high ceilings, brightened by shafts of light that filtered through a large stained-glass window on the west wall. It was furnished with a pulpit and a rostrum. Hymnals were stored in tall glass-fronted bookcases at the back of the room. A pipe organ had been purchased, and the chaplain's wife, who came on Sunday to play hymns, organized a choir of prisoners. For many prisoners, Sunday services were a highlight of the week.

The chaplain also offered classes on Sunday afternoons and scheduled individual consultations during the week to discuss moral issues. A Bible was placed in each prisoner's cell. Members of the Women's Christian Temperance Union were invited to give presentations.

Education was a priority, and a teacher held classes for illiterates and wrote letters for them to their families. She distributed textbooks on a variety of topics, everything from the alphabet to higher mathematics. A library had been established in 1875, stocked with donations from various civic groups. Its initial inventory of 400 books had increased to more than 3,000, including fiction and works about history, travel, and religion. The library distributed catalogs for prisoners to choose books to borrow, and they were encouraged to read in their cells. Several newspapers regularly donated daily copies of their publications.

By the end of the century, the penitentiary had its own newspaper—the *Anamosa Prison Press*—written almost entirely by convicts. "Local Prison Chat" was an especially popular feature. Distributed within and outside the walls, the newspaper also included national news, biographical sketches, poems, fiction, reports on the school, and essays urging prison reform. Subscriptions were available to the public at a cost of seventy-five cents a year.

8.

IT WAS LATE AFTERNOON on January 14, 1890—the day of Wesley's arrival—when he was released from the intake staff and taken to meet Warden Marquis Barr.

Barr had followed the case in the newspapers—he knew that Wesley was only eleven years old—and yet he was astonished by the boy's appearance. Given the violence of the murders, he had not expected to see such a slight and immature child standing before him. Wesley was small and frail, with delicate features and a manner that seemed almost feminine.

Barr later described that first meeting in his office:

> I cannot express my feelings when I first saw him. My heart was filled with pity and sympathy for him. . . . He looked thin, pale, and weak. . . . He had a slight twitching of the head and eyes, looked sad, when spoken to would answer promptly and intelligently, but seldom commenced a conversation. Morally, he was a mystery, and had it not been for the fact that he had pleaded guilty to a heinous crime my answer would be "morally good. I never knew him to use profane or obscene language."

Warden Barr understood that Clayton County citizens had labeled Wesley as innately evil, born without conscience or a moral sense, and irredeemable. Although he was convinced that most prisoners could be reformed, Barr also recognized that some were incorrigible, bent on a path of misconduct and criminal behavior. He wondered if Wesley Elkins, convicted of murder, would be among this group.

Barr greeted Wesley kindly, and then, hoping to assess the child's comprehension of what he had done, Barr asked him directly why he had killed his parents. In the past, Wesley had said only a few words in response to that question, but now he confided more about his childhood. He said that he had been forced to move to his father's home after his birthmother died, and that his father and stepmother had never wanted him there. He hadn't been allowed to go to school; he worked at the sawmill during the day and did chores at home in the evenings. His father and his stepmother had often punished him so much that he felt sore and bruised when he went to bed and had trouble sleeping. Sometimes at night his father sent him to the barn at night where Wesley would lie on the hay next to the animals. Once he had tried to run away, but he didn't have anywhere to go. His father had found him at a neighbor's house and had angrily taken him back to the house.

Wesley was reluctant to talk about the crime, except to say that he was sorry about what had happened. Barr didn't ask for details. He could tell that the boy knew he had done something wrong but did not comprehend the magnitude of his actions or the severity of the consequences.

Since Wesley was far younger and more vulnerable than the other prisoners, Barr decided to separate him from the hardened criminals as much as possible. He assigned the boy to do chores in the deputy warden's office, and he asked the prison chaplain to pay special attention to the young prisoner. He had no option, however, except to give Wesley a cell where he would be surrounded by adult convicts. Wesley would sleep in cell number 64 on the ground floor.

In early February, less than a month after Wesley arrived at the prison, Warden Barr allowed two men from outside the prison walls to visit the boy. A reporter from the *Anamosa Journal* wrote an article introducing Wesley to the community and relating the sad facts of his childhood. He referred to Wesley as "the little fellow" and described him as slight and fair-skinned "with a winning smile . . . and a truthful light in his dark blue eyes." In the reporter's opinion, ideas bandied about by phrenologists were "more humbug than anything else," and he poked fun at the conclusion that the shape of Wesley's head suggested innate criminal tendencies. Instead, Wesley's features indicated that he was intelligent, energetic, and friendly.

> We can pick out a hundred persons in Anamosa whose facial and cranial contour is not as favorable as this boy's. And there are members of the United States Supreme Court and ministers of the gospel whose craniums bear the indices of destructiveness and combativeness just as strongly.

The other visitor was Reverend S. S. Hunting, a former minister of the Unitarian church in Des Moines and the president of the Iowa Prisoners' Aid Association. At the age of sixty-five, Hunting had taken up the cause of prison reform and had spoken widely about the need to educate and rehabilitate those behind bars. When he spoke to Wesley, he tried to understand the boy's motive. Wesley again talked about the harsh treatment he had received from his father and stepmother. Sometimes, he said, he would lie in bed comforting himself with thoughts of escape. His father's rifle hung on the wall in front of him, and he often stared at it and imagined shooting his father. One night, he said, he was suffering from a bad headache, and he must have lost control.

As Reverend Hunting listened to the story, he was struck by Wesley's naiveté. Hunting saw him as a child who had been neglected and mistreated and whose crime should be attributed to the suffering he had endured. In Hunting's opinion, Wesley should have been sent to a reformatory with other juveniles, where he could be educated and instructed in spiritual and moral matters. The minister thought that a child as young as Wesley had the potential to mature into a law-abiding adult and deserved to be given that chance.

Over the next two years, Warden Barr spent many hours talking to the boy, and he reached the same conclusion. While Wesley was smart and eager to learn from others, he struck Barr as "a child who had been sadly neglected and perhaps had received harsh treatment, all of which might have caused him to become morose and revengeful." Wesley, Barr believed, would benefit from kind-hearted treatment and adult guidance, both of which had been lacking during his childhood. Barr sought to impress upon Wesley the enormity of what he had done, while also encouraging him and giving him hope about his future.

It was imperative, he said, that Wesley strive to obey the rules, focus on his education, and control his impulses. He must devote himself to becoming a contributing member of the prison community; show by his demeanor and behavior that he understood the difference between right and wrong; and demonstrate that he was not a threat to society.

With a message that would motivate Wesley for the rest of his life, Barr told the young and impressionable boy that if he were successful, he would eventually earn his release from prison and live as a free man. He should recognize that Clayton County citizens might always judge him as malevolent and immoral. It was up to Wesley to prove that they were wrong.

9.

DAYS FOR THE PRISONERS at Anamosa Penitentiary began at 5:30 A.M. with the loud clanging of bells in the south cellblock. The cells were small—about 40 square feet in size and 7 feet high—with heavy iron doors that stayed locked through the night. The walls and ceilings of each cell, as well as the partitions between them, were stone. Two men were assigned to each space, where they slept in narrow iron bunk beds outfitted with straw-tick mattresses and straw-filled pillows. In addition to the beds, prisoners were provided with two wooden stools, two wooden boxes called kneelers for the storage of personal items, a small table, two tin cups, two hand towels, a shaving mirror, and a Bible. The prison had electric light until 9 P.M., but there was no plumbing or running water in the cellblock. The men used toilet buckets that stood in the corner of each cell.

After they were awakened by the bells, the men rose, straightened their beds, and washed, using basins and water pitchers. Convicts who had recently arrived, or who were guilty of misbehavior, were required to eat in their cells. The others waited until the individual iron doors were unlocked and then formed a single-file line to walk to the dining hall. Each man extended his right arm and placed his hand on the shoulder of the man in front; they each carried a toilet bucket in their left hand. Talking was not permitted, and under the watch of guards with wooden truncheons, they trudged to the yard to dump the contents of the buckets in the sewer. Then, still in lockstep, they headed inside the building for breakfast.

The dining hall was designed to seat 400 men. At the front and back, guards stood or sat on stools, with spittoons conveniently placed on the floor next to them. Prisoners served the food and cleared and washed the dishes. A typical breakfast consisted of coffee, bread, and a bean or potato stew; occasionally, oatmeal and fried sausage were served. A rule of silence was strictly enforced, and prisoners who wanted something—an extra slice of bread, more coffee—used established hand signals to communicate to the waiters.

A bell marked the end of the meal, and the prisoners again formed rows to march to their various work details. Many men were on construction crews, renovating and repairing existing buildings or working on new ones. Others planted and harvested crops in the large prison garden, which included a greenhouse, and some took care of the livestock: pigs—housed in a 2,300-square-foot hog confinement—and cattle. Some prisoners were assigned to the power plant that generated electricity for the prison and to the four large boilers that produced the steam necessary for heating the various buildings. Men worked in the kitchen and in the dining hall—cooking, serving, and washing up—and others joined cleaning crews elsewhere. The prison had a carpentry shop and a machine shop; a laundry; and a bathhouse with hot and cold running water. Men were trained to be tailors and barbers and to work in the hospital, which was staffed with a full-time doctor to provide care for the sick and injured.

Convicts who could be trusted outside the prison walls traveled to the quarry, and they had the most perilous and exhausting jobs. Their work started at the stone shed, where they were chained together and loaded into empty railroad cars for the two-mile trip. At the quarry, they were armed with heavy tools, including hand saws, sledgehammers, and crow bars, and then they mounted the steep inclines to cut and pry the limestone away from the sides. The large blocks were extracted and lifted by hoists to the bottom of the quarry, where they were cut into smaller pieces and loaded onto railroad cars. Throughout the day, the cars traveled back and forth between the quarry and the shed, running on tracks across the main prison yard. At the shed, men unloaded and stacked the stone, while others worked inside. The limestone had hardened significantly by the time it reached the stonecutters. Using mallets, chisels, square-tooth axes, and bush hammers, the men exerted considerable force and skill to shape the blocks into oblongs suitable for building. More than a few of these workers had been injured by a sharp tool that missed its mark.

Prisoners working construction inside the complex were also at serious risk of getting hurt. Three men were killed and two badly hurt in one of the worst accidents just before Christmas in 1891, less than two years after Wesley had arrived. The five men were building a roof support for the new Female Department, and they were standing on a temporary wooden platform five stories above the ground. A heavy stone slab lay on the platform, and a guard ordered that no more be loaded on. When the guard turned his back, the convicts, hoping to make the job go faster, disobeyed. They hoisted up another block, and the weight of the stone—totaling more than one ton—caused the platform to collapse. Four of the men plunged to the ground along with the load of stone; three suffered fatal injuries and a fourth was severely injured and crippled for life. The other survivor—a young man serving a three-year sentence for burning down his own store to claim the insurance money—miraculously escaped death by grabbing an iron beam on the fourth floor, and then inching his way along the beam to a window ledge. In a sad twist of irony, one of the dead men had been scheduled for release within a few days. When he died, the official pardon notice from the governor was waiting in the warden's office, along with a letter from his mother expressing her joy at his imminent return home.

10.

IN JANUARY 1892, Marquis Barr, who had served six years, left his position as warden of the penitentiary. No one denied that his leadership had been excellent, but many state legislators thought that it was time for a change.

On April 1, 1892, Philander Madden began his term at Anamosa, now home to 262 prisoners. Madden's background was remarkably similar to Barr's: he had enlisted in the Union Army as a young man and was then elected sheriff of Clay County, located 260 miles from Anamosa. Like Barr, he had a large family, including his wife and six children ranging in age from six to fifteen.

Warden Madden was more casual and less careful in supervising the operations of the penitentiary than Barr had been. He was a good-natured man, and it was generally agreed that he could be friendly to a fault. "HAPPY ARE THE CONVICTS AT ANAMOSA PRISON" read the headline in one newspaper article, reporting that men were rarely penalized for disobeying the rules and were often seen freely congregating in the yards. In the evenings, some of them gathered in an unused building where they played cards, smoked, and cooked food on a two-burner stove. Madden occasionally joined them for a hand or two of poker. When it was reported that some convicts had weapons and tools hidden in their cells, Anamosa citizens grew increasingly concerned about the possibility of escape attempts.

Warden Madden seemed unfazed by the reports. He enjoyed fraternizing with the prisoners, and he believed that his goal was to prepare them to rejoin society.

Madden knew about Wesley, the youngest prisoner at thirteen years of age, and Barr had told him that he was pleased by the boy's good record of behavior and moral growth. Wesley was obedient, well-mannered, and attentive to lessons, and he was making progress on the path to reform. Given the report from Barr, Madden hadn't expected trouble from Wesley, and he was surprised one evening to hear that Wesley was missing from his cell at the night count. Electric lights were turned on to illuminate the main yard, where the guards found him hiding alone. Prisoners who were attempting to escape sometimes used blankets twisted into ropes to scale the walls, but Wesley carried nothing that indicated such a plan. The disobedience was out of character for Wesley. It seemed more like a childish act than an escape attempt.

Warden Madden decided not to consider the incident as a serious offense, and he reprimanded Wesley in private. He was concerned about the boy, and he worried about how he was treated by other prisoners. Guards had reported that Wesley appeared to be easily hurt by teasing from the older criminals. For a brief period, Wesley had worked at a stall selling trinkets to visitors inside the prison complex, and a convict had bragged about how he tricked the unsuspecting boy into accepting five counterfeit nickels.

Madden followed Barr's lead, separating Wesley from others as much as possible. He assigned the boy to the prison library, a large and bright room furnished with rows of tall wooden bookshelves, tables, and chairs. Although Wesley would be by himself much of the time, its location—near the chapel and the schoolroom on the second floor of the main building—would assure frequent contact with the chaplain and the teacher. Madden understood that Wesley had already become a good reader, and this job would give him a chance to make up for the schooling he had been denied as a child.

With the increasing emphasis on literacy, the library played a vital role at the prison, and Wesley was given significant responsibilities. Already stocked with more than 3,000 books, the library was still increasing its inventory, receiving books from townspeople and purchasing others, and Wesley would be in charge of cataloging and shelving them. He would also record loans to prisoners, who could request two volumes a week. Roughly a thousand books, magazines, and newspapers were checked out to members of the prison population during a typical month. The decision by Warden Madden affected the course of Wesley's life. It proved to be a perfect fit for the young boy. According to Madden:

> [Wesley] speedily developed a deep love for the books with which he was surrounded, and every moment of his time not occupied with his duties as librarian was dedicated to the close perusal of such works as he was then able to master intelligently. Encouraged and assisted by the prison chaplain and others, his progress in this connection was nothing less than phenomenal.

Wesley became a serious student, and he read widely from the collection. He impressed officials at Anamosa with his eagerness and quick ability to learn, traits that were remarkable to his supporters in later years. He read books on history as well as classic works of literature. His favorite writers were Rudyard Kipling and Robert Louis Stevenson, both popular authors of the era. Kipling's books and short stories told exotic tales set in distant India, and they must have thrilled the imagination of the boy who had seen nothing of the world except for rural Iowa and the inside of a penitentiary. Stevenson's novels—*Treasure Island*, an adventure story of pirates and gold treasure, and *Kidnapped*, the saga of a young orphan boy destined to find his own way in the world—appealed to many young people of Wesley's generation.

It is likely that Wesley also read one of Stevenson's darker and more disturbing tales, the short novel titled *The Strange Case of Dr. Jekyll and Mr. Hyde*, which portrays the intense psychological battle between good and evil in its main character. The notion that evil might be concealed in the guise of innocence was exactly what many citizens in Clayton County believed about Wesley.

The library contained a few shelves of legal volumes, including Iowa statutes and court decisions. Some of the more educated prisoners spent time researching their appeals, and they shared information with others. In the fall of 1892, when Wesley was fourteen, he received a tip from one of the prisoners who had found a published opinion from the Iowa Supreme Court in 1878. The case—*State v. Fowler*—looked like it might be a favorable precedent.

The facts were simple enough. During recess, a schoolboy named Silas Fowler had used a slingshot to fire a rock at George Reith, a classmate. The rock struck Reith on the head, and Reith suffered a slight but bloody wound. Fowler was indicted, convicted of assault, and fined $25 and court costs. His lawyers appealed his conviction to the Iowa Supreme Court, arguing on six separate grounds. Only one was relevant to Wesley.

The significance to Wesley came from a legal principle quoted in the case, which was accepted by all parties as an accurate statement of the law. The judge and the lawyers on both sides—prosecution and defense—agreed that, under common law, a child between the ages of seven and fourteen must be presumed to be incapable of committing any crime. The presumption could be rebutted only if the state could prove that the child had sufficient capacity to comprehend what he had done. Without such convincing proof, a child of fourteen or younger had to be acquitted.

Accordingly, whenever the defendant was fourteen or younger, the jury had to be instructed to apply the rule. In the *Fowler* case, however, the judge had refused the defense lawyer's request to give the instruction, declaring that the defendant's age was proven to be fifteen so that the common law rule was irrelevant.

On appeal, the Iowa Supreme Court disagreed with the lower court, holding that the defendant's age was a question for the jury.

Given the conflicting evidence, the jury could find that Fowler was younger than fifteen, and then it would be obliged to consider the presumption of innocence. According to the Court, the judge's refusal to give the proper instruction was reversible error, and the case was sent back for retrial.

The common law rule had been well established years before Wesley pled guilty to the murders of his parents. While lawyers in other cases had raised the "infancy defense" on behalf of their young clients—relying on the presumption that a child should be acquitted—James Crosby, the lawyer assigned to defend Wesley, had never cited that rule.

Although there was little doubt that Wesley had killed his parents, Crosby might have challenged the confession attributed to Wesley as insufficient evidence of malice aforethought. Wesley was an uneducated child at the time, and yet the statement produced by James Corlett was meticulous and exhaustive, written as a lengthy monologue. The extensive details might have been added by Corlett, and even if Wesley had acknowledged some of the specifics, he may have been responding to leading questions from Corlett. After all, Wesley was alone in the buggy with the man at the time he admitted his guilt, and Corlett's account was the only evidence that the boy had acted with criminal intent. Should that have been sufficient to overcome the presumption of innocence? James Crosby had not raised that question.

In a later statement to a reporter, Crosby declared that he had concluded almost immediately that Wesley "had murder in his heart," and would engage in his "murderous propensity at the least provocation." Crosby, like the rest of the community, was so appalled by the crime that, by the time of the trial, he was convinced that life imprisonment was the only appropriate punishment. Crosby had ignored the fact that Wesley was an eleven-year-old child.

After reading *State v. Fowler*, Wesley understood that ineffective counsel could be a basis for release from prison. A petition would have to be filed with a federal court, setting forth the grounds and asking for a writ of habeas corpus, a long-established protection against unlawful detention. A few prisoners, often with financial help from their families, had hired outside lawyers to pursue their appeals, and Wesley saw that as his best chance. He had saved the pittance he had earned from his labor over the last three years, and he went directly to Warden Madden with his request.

Madden wasn't sure how to proceed. In October 1892, he wrote to Governor Horace Boies for advice. Explaining that Wesley had discovered an Iowa decision that seemed applicable to his case, Madden wrote that the boy "desires to employ an attorney to investigate this matter and has placed twenty dollars in our hands with instructions to send it to an attorney to aid him. He thinks he can get out on a writ of habeas corpus. What shall I do about it?"

Whether or not the governor responded, Wesley was not provided with legal counsel. No one told Wesley that a petition—filed more than a year after he was imprisoned—would probably have been dismissed as untimely. Although Wesley must have accepted that habeas corpus was not his path to freedom, he did not forget the suggestion that his conviction and life sentence were unjust.

11.

WESLEY SOON LEARNED that convicts sentenced to life in prison had only one path to freedom. The governor could release these prisoners only after the General Assembly had debated the issue. Under the Iowa Constitution, the governor received applications from prisoners, and, in most cases, he could decide on his own to issue a parole or pardon, or to commute a sentence. The process was different for those convicts serving life sentences. When the governor received their applications, he had two choices: he could deny the request on his own, or if he were inclined to consider a prisoner's release, he was required to seek advice from the General Assembly. After discussions, legislators would vote on the question. These prisoners were not traditionally paroled, and the General Assembly would advise the governor either to pardon the applicant or to keep the lifer behind bars. Although the governor was not required to follow the advice, he typically felt compelled to do so.

Freeing a convicted murderer was sure to trigger strong feelings, and the statute was designed to assure that the public had an opportunity to share their views with their representatives. If a governor chose to ask for advice from legislators, he had to request that two different newspapers—one in Des Moines and one in the county where the trial had been held—published announcements for four consecutive weeks, informing the public that the case would be considered by the next General Assembly. The final notice had to appear at least twenty days before the legislature began its session.

The Iowa General Assembly convened only once every two years. Its session began in early January of even-numbered years, a few days before the newly elected governor was inaugurated for his two-year term. To allow time for public notice before legislative review, convicted murderers filed their applications for pardon in mid-November of odd-numbered years, giving the governor time to decide whether to forward the request to the legislature. The governor reviewed applications and listened to appeals from outsiders and family members. As reported by the *Cedar Rapids Republican* in the fall of 1895:

> It is not an unusual occurrence for the chief executive . . . to find some poor broken-hearted wife or mother at his door waiting for him when he comes downstairs in the morning. She throws herself at his feet, and with many tears begs for the life of her son or husband. No one but a stoic can go through such ordeals unmoved.

Favorable public opinion was important to an applicant's success in the General Assembly. Assurance that a released prisoner would have financial support and a stable home environment could be persuasive. Proof of special skills in a trade was also a strong positive factor, as were educational progress and support from community members. Prisoners sometimes persuaded influential citizens to speak on their behalf. They hoped that a senator or representative would take up their cause on the floor of the capitol.

The General Assembly discussed applications from convicted murderers in the spring of even-numbered years and communicated its recommendations to the governor, who would make the final decision. Sometimes two different governors were involved in the process. The outgoing governor would take the first step in November, deciding which applications would be rejected and which would be considered by the General Assembly. The newly elected governor, however, would be the one signing the official pardon papers in the spring.

Typically, a governor would receive fifteen or twenty such pardon requests from convicted murderers, and few were granted. By 1895, more than twenty years after the law was passed, only eleven convicted murderers, a small percentage of those who applied, had been released. In late 1893, for example, the outgoing governor, Horace Boies, forwarded ten applications to the General Assembly, and only one man—Thomas Brooks—received the positive support of the legislators. Brooks, whose parents were highly respected in their community, had killed a man in a saloon fight. The victim was said to be of bad character, and numerous petitions in favor of Brooks's release had been signed by citizens of his community, including all members of the jury that convicted him. Warden Madden had been in charge when Brooks walked away from Anamosa Penitentiary as a free man.

Outside support had been crucial in Brooks's case, and Madden, who was sympathetic to Wesley, knew no one who would speak publicly on Wesley's behalf. Perhaps it was Madden who suggested that Wesley write to Carl Snyder, the editor of the *Council Bluffs Nonpareil.* In 1890, after Wesley had been sentenced to life in prison, Snyder had published editorials excoriating the legal system for convicting such a young boy for murder, and he had continued to be an outspoken proponent of prison reform. When Snyder published an editorial in 1895 advocating for more effective methods of rehabilitating convicts, Wesley wrote to him directly to appeal for his help. Unfortunately, this letter does not exist in the archives.

Carl Snyder was twenty-six years old. He had been born into a prominent and financially secure family, and he had enjoyed the benefits of higher education, graduating from the University of Iowa. His father was a well-known newspaper man who had worked as an editor in Cedar Rapids and a publisher in Red Oak before moving to the far western border of the state and purchasing the *Nonpareil.* As the paper's manager, he had convinced his son to move there and assume the top editorial spot. Once in that job, Carl Snyder published his own opinion pieces, and he became known for his sharp intelligence, aggressive style, and strong opinions. He was skilled as a journalist, and he had broad intellectual interests. Fluent in several languages, Snyder was a serious student in the fields of science, history, and moral philosophy. People in Council Bluffs and elsewhere in the state saw him as an exceptionally talented and ambitious young man, and he had always set his sights high.

Within a few years, Snyder would leave Iowa to travel and study in Europe before moving permanently to the East Coast, where he would write editorials for the *Washington Post.* He would go on to be a renowned economic statistician at the Federal Reserve Bank of New York. But in 1895, when he heard from Wesley, Snyder was a young journalist at the start of his career, and he was eager to express his positions on issues he deemed important to social policy.

At the time Wesley wrote to Snyder, he could not have guessed how significant the contact would prove to be. Snyder reacted to Wesley's letter with sympathy and compassion. As Snyder had asserted in his editorials when he first heard about the case, he was appalled that an eleven-year-old child could be thought capable of criminal intent and sent to prison for life. Snyder immediately wrote back to Wesley, asking for more details about his life, and the two began a correspondence. Initiating his own investigation into the case, Snyder contacted people who had known Wesley in Clayton County and others who had observed his progress at Anamosa. Nothing he heard changed his view that Wesley's imprisonment was morally wrong.

12.

WESLEY WAS SEVENTEEN in the fall of 1895 when he made his first appeal for freedom, addressed to Governor Frank D. Jackson. It was brief and formal:

> Sir:
>
> Being a prisoner confined in the State Penitentiary at Anamosa, Iowa, and serving a life sentence for the crime of murder in the first degree, I wish to state that I have been already confined in said prison for the period of nearly six years and that a petition to your excellency and to the Members of the General Assembly for commutation of my sentence to fifteen years, will be forwarded to you, which I pray you to lay before the General Assembly, for their action thereon.
>
> I was tried and sentenced at the January term 1890, of the District Court of Clayton County, Judge Hoyt presiding.
>
> Most respectfully yours, John W. Elkins

Although most lifers requested pardons from the governor, Wesley did not ask for immediate release, and he did not plead his case or present a defense. If the governor had granted his request, Wesley would have nine years left in prison.

Knowing that Carl Snyder was sympathetic to his cause, Wesley wrote to tell him what he had done. Although Snyder was vacationing on the West Coast near Puget Sound, he didn't hesitate to intervene with Governor Jackson. The two men were acquainted with each other, and Snyder considered Jackson to be a friend. In a letter dated November 1895, Snyder told the governor that he had investigated the case and was horrified at the injustice that a child should be behind bars. In Snyder's mind, commuting the sentence was "palpably absurd," and the only justifiable action for the governor would be to issue a complete pardon. Snyder was convinced that convicting such a young boy for murder was wrong as a matter of law. He appealed to the governor to consider the case not just because of Wesley, but because of the appalling precedent that would otherwise be set in the state.

Not one to mince words, Snyder wrote:

No sane man will hold that a child of 11 years is morally responsible for such a deed as this boy committed.

The idea, therefore, that an adequate *punishment* is to be meted out, and that this is to be fixed at 15 years, is offensive and disgraceful. It is a bungling notion that a child can be treated as a felon and a convict.

The only thing to be determined in this case, is whether this boy should be set free or not; whether it is wise and just and proper. . . .

I know that you are a man of positive convictions and time-worn actions as opposed to all the miserable stiffly, shilly-shallying that masquerades under the name of that which is politic and expedient. And I know that if you find time to investigate this case, you will set it before the legislature in its proper light.

Snyder must have shared his views with Wesley. Two weeks after requesting that his sentence be reduced, Wesley wrote again to the governor, this time asking for an unconditional pardon. He noted that he was only eleven years of age when he committed the crime, and that the six years he had spent in prison were sufficient punishment for the crime.

When he received the letters about Wesley's case in November, Governor Jackson was at the end of his term. He knew that he would not be making the final decision to pardon Wesley or other convicted murderers. Francis Drake was due to be inaugurated in January, and he would be the one to sign any papers granting them their freedom. Jackson had received ten applications from convicted murderers, and he decided to forward all ten to the General Assembly for its review. The *Iowa State Register*, printed in Des Moines, and the *McGregor News*, out of Clayton County, agreed to publish the required notices of the appeals from Wesley Elkins.

Although people in Clayton County had not heard much about Wesley Elkins in the six years since he had been convicted, they had not forgotten about him. When they discovered that Carl Snyder had taken up Wesley's cause, they did not take well to the news. They were angry that someone at such a distance—across the state in Council Bluffs—was interfering in a decision made by a Clayton County judge for a crime that had occurred in their midst.

Clayton County citizens already had reason to feel isolated from other Iowans. Located in the northeast corner of Iowa, the county was made up of farms linked to small towns, and without a true metropolitan area. The area was largely populated by German immigrants, and its politics made it unique as one of the few Democratic counties in a state generally controlled by Republicans. Often in the minority, its representatives spoke for constituents who strongly opposed various state policies and directives. Residents of Clayton County, for instance, had resisted the Republican initiative to pass prohibition laws. In June 1882, they held an Anti-Prohibition Convention with Robert Quigley, future county attorney, serving as chairman of the gathering. When prohibition laws were enacted at the state level, enforcement efforts in Clayton County generated heated controversy and hostility, and saloons and breweries continued to operate in defiance of the state government.

Residents felt just as strongly about their rights to make decisions about local crimes. In the same year that John and Hattie Elkins had been killed, there was another homicide in the county.

J. J. Grinnell, a well-liked individual who served as the county recorder, had discovered that his wife had been intimate in the past with Gregory Cornell, an engineer on the Milwaukee Road railroad. When Grinnell discovered that the affair was ongoing, he shot Cornell in a hotel lobby in downtown McGregor. Many people had observed the shooting, and the facts were not in dispute. Grinnell was arrested and tried. Despite evidence that he had premeditated the crime, he was acquitted. Sentiment was strongly in favor of Grinnell, and in a verdict that pleased the public, the jury decided that Grinnell had gone temporarily insane upon seeing Cornell in town.

In contrast, Clayton County residents had little compassion for Wesley Elkins. According to the confession they had read, the boy had planned his crime, attacked his parents while they slept, and then lied to his neighbors and investigators in order to hide his tracks. Rumors about his mother's murderous nature had convinced them that Wesley had inherited immutable and dangerous traits from her. Their elected officials had investigated the case, and their judge had convicted and sentenced him. Not even Wesley's lawyer had been able to come up with a defense for his actions. People in Clayton County were satisfied with the decision that Wesley was guilty of first-degree murder and should be kept in prison for life. In their minds, they were entitled to decide Wesley's fate.

Within a few days after the initial notice appeared in the newspaper, the *Cedar Rapids Republican* published a story headlined "ELKINS WANTS A PARDON." The inflammatory article, which characterized Wesley as one of the "most famous criminals in the state," included details that had been fabricated to dramatize the story.

Three days later, the *Republican* ran a long editorial, repeating statements from the article and strongly advocating against a pardon for Wesley, describing him in monstrous and damning terms. Although the paper called Carl Snyder a "brilliant newspaper correspondent," it harshly criticized him for arguing on behalf of Wesley Elkins. According to the editorial, Snyder's sympathy was dangerously misplaced, and he was badly mistaken in thinking that Wesley had been transformed by his education. Snyder may have corresponded with Wesley, but he had not met him in person or spoken to him directly. People in Clayton County claimed to know the boy better than Snyder did, and they were certain that Wesley was immune to any cultivating influence, and that efforts to rehabilitate him were destined to fail.

The *Republican* cited a man, identified as one of Clayton County's "most distinguished citizens," as an authority on the boy's evil tendencies. The source—later identified as Wesley's own defense lawyer, James Crosby—had agreed to a lengthy interview. Crosby, of course, had persuaded Wesley to plead guilty, and he approved the conviction of first-degree murder and the life sentence. Now he took the opportunity to justify his actions, claiming to know about incidents that were never corroborated or repeated by anyone. There was no factual basis to Crosby's story, and yet his account formed the basis of the *Republican*'s indictment of Wesley.

Although Wesley's classmates later disputed the claims, Crosby asserted that Wesley had terrorized them, and that they had feared and avoided the young boy. According to Crosby, Wesley had nearly killed his older brother by throwing an axe at him. As additional evidence of Wesley's criminal impulse, Crosby declared that Wesley had been provoked to kill his parents by a slight scolding from his father, and that, once in prison, he had continued his violent ways. Crosby cited his own conversations with Wesley to prove that the boy was evil, describing Wesley's tone as one of "supreme indifference . . . never displaying any human feeling whatever." No testimonials from prison or letters from Wesley would ever persuade Crosby to change his mind: he was convinced that Wesley was a diabolical criminal and that releasing him from prison would have dire consequences.

The editor of the *Republican* offered his own assessment of Wesley Elkins:

> This fiend of a boy has never realized the enormity of his crime. He speaks of it as one would speak of the most common event, without a tear or a shadow of remorse. Since he has been confined at Anamosa, he has attempted numerous assaults.
>
> It is evident that through some cause—we know not what— this boy is possessed with a passion to kill. He cannot, ought not, be released. He should be treated kindly, educated and given a chance to earn something, but he should not be set at liberty. The chances are too desperate. . . . Wesley Elkins is one of the most remarkable criminals in the United States. Every fact relative to his history, including his prenatal history, ought to be known, both as a lesson and as a warning.

The points outlined in the newspaper—Wesley's genetic disposition to criminality, dispassionate reflection on the horror of the crime, and potential for future violence—would form the essence of the Clayton County argument against the pardon. This characterization of Wesley would be repeated many times in the years to come.

ISOLATED FROM SOCIETY since he was a child, Wesley could not have anticipated the vehement reaction to his appeal. He was taken aback by the lies included in the depiction of him as a monster, and he responded with a five-page handwritten letter addressed to the editor of the *Republican.*

Wesley objected to the account of his childhood from the anonymous source, calling it "one mass of falsehood from beginning to end, which was brought out by prejudice and passion with hardly a word of truth in it." He refuted each specific charge, denying reports that his schoolmates had ever been afraid of him. His teachers, he said, would testify that he had "as many true and good friends as anyone else in school." He had never thrown an axe at his brother, nor had he attacked anyone at Anamosa. Prison officials and guards, he said, would confirm his exemplary record there.

Wesley also disputed that he had been provoked by a mere scolding from his parents. He had confided his account previously to Warden Barr, and now he was willing to share it with others:

If my father and stepmother had treated me in any degree kindly, I would not be behind these walls today. I can appreciate kindness wherever it is found, in the high or low, but they were cruel in the extreme: many a night I have been sent to my bed, with my back so sore from a whipping, that I could not lay on it; and at the time of my arrest, I could of showed black and blue marks on my body, brought on by not doing a piece of work to suit my stepmother; but which I done to the best of my ability; and, goaded on by such treatment, which I did not deserve, I committed the rash deed that, too young to realize it at that time, I do now and shall always deplore it to the end of my days. . . .

Wesley appealed to the editor of the *Republican* for his support, and asked that he print a retraction:

With these facts before you, I ask you, as a reasonable man, if there is a shadow of a cause why I should be punished further?

I have been all my lifetime, I might say, in prison; I came here at eleven years of age, never realizing the enormity of the crime I did at the time, nor until about two years after imprisonment here, when it came gradually upon me; when I awoke to the full realization of the crime that I had done; and today, there is nothing in my past life, or ever will be in the future that I do, or ever will deplore more, than the memory of that deed.

My case is going before the coming legislature, and I hope, as I have endeavored to lay the truth before you and deny the false charges against me, that your paper will do me justice, and correct the error of this edition; I cannot hope to cope with the press; I can only appeal to your manhood and sense of justice.

Warden Madden read the letter before Wesley was permitted to send it. Although the warden understood Wesley's distress, he was concerned that the newspaper might respond by repeating the false attacks, attracting more public attention and damaging Wesley's future chances for release.

Wesley agreed to Madden's suggestion that he should write directly to Governor Jackson instead of the newspaper. Enclosing the handwritten letter addressed to the editor of the *Republican*, he asked the governor to communicate his concerns to the General Assembly.

There is no record that the governor did that, or that legislators were ever aware of Wesley's letter refuting the false claims.

13.

ON DECEMBER 16, 1895, a new prisoner, Charles Curtis, arrived at Anamosa Penitentiary. After two women testified that they were married to Curtis in that year, he had been convicted of the crime of bigamy. He was sentenced to five years of hard labor by Judge Thompson in the Jones County District Court. The following year, in 1896, a third woman would come forward to claim that she had also been married to Curtis in 1895.

At the time of his incarceration, Curtis was a resident of the town of Anamosa and was already acquainted with several of the guards. He had worked in the newspaper business for several years. Upon his arrival, he was bathed, weighed, measured for clothes, given the traditional prisoner haircut, and assigned identity number "3247." He turned over his assets—what Curtis wryly referred to as "his wealth"—which totaled eight cents. Oddly enough for a man convicted of bigamy, the Convict Register listed his marital status as "Single."

Although the transition from free man to prisoner was understandably traumatic, the pain for Curtis was cushioned by the fact that he was—in his own words—"full of opium" when he arrived at the penitentiary. He had somehow smuggled enough of the drug into the prison to avoid immediate symptoms of withdrawal—he later claimed he had not been thoroughly searched—but from then on, his primary concern was how to maintain his drug habit. Before long, he was selling his few possessions: a coat and vest to a fellow convict; an overcoat to the son of a guard; and "a fine pair of five-dollar shoes" to another guard. He borrowed two dollars from his attorney. All the cash went toward his opium addiction. He made connections with a trusty—a prisoner who had special privileges and contacts with outside sources—who supplied him with the drug. By early April, though, Curtis was out of cash. He admitted his addiction to Doctor Dwight Sigworth, the prison physician, who agreed to help Curtis go through a detoxification regimen. Curtis suffered from the withdrawal, and his weight dropped from 135 pounds to 111 pounds, but he had kicked his habit by the end of the summer.

As a man in the newspaper business, Curtis prided himself on his writing skills, and he wanted to get his name before the public. He wrote a lengthy account of daily life at Anamosa, and he was pleased when a newspaper in Minnesota agreed to publish it. Before he was released from prison, he expanded the letter into an entertaining memoir titled "Five Years at Anamosa," which also included a long depiction of his life before prison and the many injustices he had suffered during his incarceration. He claimed, however, that he had another goal. As he wrote: "Should the little story convince one young man or young woman that there is a need of living a better and purer life; then the hours of pain which have made these words a personal experience will not have been in vain." He also admitted to a second motivation: he hoped that sales of the book would bring him sufficient money to meet his financial needs.

Curtis was always pleased by the attention he attracted from visitors. He was proud to admit in his memoir that visitors to the prison were interested to gawk and stare at "the man with forty wives," and that a guard had once warned women not to stare at the bigamist or she might end up married to him.

Curtis also bragged about the large number of visitors who paid to tour Anamosa specifically so they could see him, and he noted that their money "undoubtedly caused the library fund to grow." As the prison librarian, Wesley would have appreciated the increased budget, and Curtis, an educated man, would have enjoyed examining the new books.

As a journalist, Curtis would have known about the sensation caused by the Elkins case several years earlier, and to him, Wesley must have seemed like a celebrity. Always curious about goings on inside and outside the prison, Curtis would have made the acquaintance of Wesley. Several years later, the two men worked together, giving them an opportunity to form a closer bond.

The names of the prisoners serving life sentences were well known among the convicts at Anamosa, who applauded and cheered for those who applied for pardon. We don't know whether Wesley discussed his appeal with Curtis, but certainly Curtis recognized that the spring of 1896 would be an anxious time for the young man in the library.

IN EARLY JANUARY, the twenty-sixth biannual meeting of the Iowa State Legislature assembled in Des Moines for the inauguration of the newly elected governor, Francis Drake. Governor Drake was sixty-five years old, a former Brigadier General with the 36th Iowa Volunteer Infantry and the founder of Drake University. He would serve only a single term in office.

Legislators spent the first few months of the session considering proposed legislation. They stipulated life imprisonment for any male who had sexual relations with an underage female and raised the age of consent from thirteen to fifteen. They discussed whether pharmacists should be allowed to sell malt liquors, and passed a law outlawing the sale of cigarettes or cigarette papers in the state. There was a lengthy debate about women's right to vote in general elections. At the end of February, the women's suffrage bill was defeated 49 to 44.

Discussions about the ten appeals for pardon were delayed until the final month of the session after the Senate Committees on Penitentiaries and Pardons had completed their review. The one from Wesley Elkins had attracted public attention, but he was not the most prominent applicant. In the spring of 1896, that honor belonged to the notorious Charles Polk Wells, whose name and exploits were legendary in the still-untamed West of the late nineteenth century. Wells had been an Indian fighter with Kit Carson and an outlaw with the Jesse James and Cole Younger gangs. He was originally tried for highway robbery, having allegedly robbed at least two express trains and three banks. He was shot three times before he was captured, and, at his trial, he was sentenced to ten years at Fort Madison. Wells had tried unsuccessfully to escape from prison, and, during the attempt, he and two accomplices killed a guard with chloroform, earning a life sentence for that crime. He extolled his exploits and escapes in a short book he wrote in prison titled *The Life and Adventure of Polk Wells*.

In his application for pardon, Wells pled his case. He and his two accomplices had only intended to disable the guard, not to kill him, and the other men, who were just as guilty as he was, had already been released. He had served fifteen years, which seemed sufficient punishment for his crimes, particularly since he was suffering from tuberculosis and other ailments. During his years in prison, Wells claimed, he had found religion. If he were released, he would live quietly with his sister in Fort Madison. Although he knew he could leverage his notoriety to make money, he pledged that he would not go on the lecture circuit to talk about his exploits.

Many people were astonished when the Committees on Pardons recommended that Wells be pardoned, and his case excited interest throughout Iowa. Several prominent men had spoken out on his behalf before his case reached the floor of the capitol, and a standing-room–only crowd listened to the vigorous debates and fiery speeches. To the disappointment of some and the relief of others, members of both the House and the Senate voted overwhelmingly against releasing Wells, and he was returned to his cell at Fort Madison.

In contrast to the frenzied publicity surrounding Wells, little attention was paid to Wesley that spring. The House Committee on Pardons considered and rejected Wesley's request so that it would not be debated on the floor. Citing the meager showing of facts, the Committee recommended that the appeal be indefinitely postponed without prejudice. The decision was reported in the newspapers.

Although Wesley Elkins and Polk Wells would remain behind bars, three lifers were given their freedom that spring. George Trout was a gambler from Sioux City who had killed a fellow gambler in a dispute over a woman and served ten years in prison. Outside supporters argued that he should have been sentenced for manslaughter instead of murder, and legislators were convinced. A. F. Hockett of Mahaska was also pardoned after eleven years in prison. When he was twenty-five years old, Hockett had been convicted of hunting down and shooting at close range a young man who had seduced Hockett's fifteen-year-old sister. Although Hockett had admitted to the violent crime—he had shot the victim and then stomped on the body—an overwhelming majority of legislators took the position that the circumstances of his crime were a mitigating factor; he was, after all, intent on protecting the honor of his sister.

The third man pardoned that year was sixty-seven-year-old William Slowey. Based on the testimony of his wife and a neighbor, Slowey had been convicted of choking a traveling salesman and leaving him to die in a barn. Years later, the neighbor confessed from his deathbed that he and Slowey's wife had killed the man accidently while they were attempting to steal his money. The neighbor admitted that Slowey had discovered them after they had committed the crime, and that Slowey had tried unsuccessfully to revive the victim. By the time of the neighbor's confession, Slowey had served sixteen years for a murder he didn't commit.

THE DECISION by the legislature was a setback for Wesley. Undoubtedly, he felt that the editorial in the *Cedar Rapids Republican* had prejudiced some of the committee members to vote against his application. He recognized, however, that the three men pardoned had served longer sentences for their crimes than he had and were supported by many people in their communities. Also, it was not the first time that any of them had applied for pardon; all three had been rejected in previous years.

Wesley resolved to be patient. He would have to wait more than a year and a half, until November of 1897, before he could file another appeal.

FOR THE MOST PART, the spring and early summer passed uneventfully at the penitentiary. In July, a prisoner named L. J. Meekin, who worked in the stone shed, failed to show up for work. A quick check of the prison indicated that he must have escaped the previous day, and somehow his absence had not been noticed in the night count of the convict population. Notably, he was one of the few escapees who was not recaptured and returned to the prison.

The peace and order of the institution were shattered on the evening of August 11, 1896. A guard patrolling the yard first noticed the smoke and gave the alarm. The fire had started near the bake oven directly under the kitchen and dining area, and the flames spread upward to the wooden joists and flooring. The Anamosa fire department responded in force a few minutes later, and firefighters entered the prison and attached hoses to the water works hydrants. Thick columns of black smoke made it difficult to properly direct the water streams, and a tank in the basement containing about ninety pounds of coal oil increased the danger.

At the time the fire was discovered, most of the 450 prisoners were already in their cells, and because of the direction of the wind, the cell house was not heated enough to break a single windowpane. There was, however, immense destruction elsewhere in the complex. The rapid spread of the blaze consumed the kitchen and dining areas, the chapel organ, the pews, most of the library's furniture and its collection of more than 3,000 books, 60 barrels of pork, 40 barrels of molasses, and storage containers of flour and lard. Fortunately, some flour, meat, and other food supplies in a nearby building were saved. While the prisoners slept, a temporary kitchen was established near the boiler and laundry rooms. By dawn, a breakfast had been prepared for the prisoners consisting of bread, cheese, bologna, and coffee. Plates, cups, and silverware were provided by local merchants.

For Wesley, the fire constituted a personal loss. The library, where he spent most of his waking hours, was gone, forcing a change in Wesley's life.

Although a small reading room was created, it would be two years before the library could be reestablished. In the meantime, Wesley was given another work assignment, but his duties were not recorded in the prison records.

Two weeks after the fire, the notorious Polk Wells was transferred from Fort Madison to Anamosa. His physical condition had worsened, and despite the extensive damage from the fire, it was thought that the medical facilities at Anamosa were better equipped to handle his care. The fire at Anamosa had dominated the local news for days, but now there was another story about the prison that attracted attention. The famous outlaw, Polk Wells, had arrived and was housed in the Anamosa prison hospital. Wells was a powerful figure during his days in the West, and he had always said that he wanted to die with his boots on. Now the ravages of tuberculosis had reduced him to a man who was gaunt and frail, on the precipice of death.

Wells lived sixteen days in the prison hospital and died on September 11, 1896, at the age of forty-five. His body was shipped to the medical college at St. Joseph, Missouri, where an autopsy was performed. Nearly two dozen bullets acquired during his gunfighting days were removed from his corpse.

14.

THE DEVASTATING FIRE at the prison in August 1896 required Warden Madden to institute new routines, including additional restrictions on the prison population. The loss of the chapel and library further depressed the spirits of the prisoners. Demolition of the charred sections occurred within days, and crews began to rebuild. The most pressing need was to find adequate space for cooking. Food was prepared in large vats in the temporary kitchen. For the next three months, prisoners ate meals in their cells. The new kitchen would not resume operation until Thanksgiving, and the dining room would not be completed and ready for use until May 1897.

Conditions at the prison were deteriorating. Economic hardship throughout the state had caused an increase in crime, and Anamosa was now dangerously overcrowded. The population of convicts stood at 628, more than double the number since Madden had assumed his position as warden. Cells were crowded, and some prisoners were forced to camp out in the yard. The August fire had made a bad situation even worse.

Wesley looked to books for comfort, but he was lonely and afraid. Christmas was never a happy time in the penitentiary despite the special dinner and the attempts by community members to bring holiday cheer to the prisoners. In late December 1896, eighteen-year-old Wesley Elkins wrote to Carl Snyder, the Iowa newspaper publisher who had supported his earlier application for pardon. The tone of Wesley's letter—disclosing and intimate—suggests that he had come to rely on Snyder as a friend and an ally. At the time, Wesley could not have known that this would be the first of his letters to be widely read by the public and that it would mark an important turning point in his life.

Wesley presented a picture of himself that was in stark contrast to the images conjured up by his crime. Despite his unique circumstances, he expressed deep and universal emotions: confusion and sorrow as he looked back on his tragic past; desperate anxiety and fear, as well as a glimmer of hope, as he faced his uncertain future. He did not present a legalistic argument for a pardon, nor did he refute his guilt or defend his actions. Instead, he described himself as a boy "who had not yet reached the age of reason" when he committed his crime. In the years since then, he had matured into a man with ambition and purpose, and he believed he had been "punished as far as it is necessary for the benefit of good morals." Wesley wrote of his anguish at the thought of spending the rest of his life behind bars:

In reviewing the past seven years which I have passed in this prison I can recall but few happy moments, and I ask myself, tremblingly, must it ever be thus? And how much strain will my mind stand before I shall have become a physical and mental degenerate?

My position here is a strange one. I am practically alone in my sympathies and hopes. I have cultivated self-reliance, and some may deem me cold, but my distant demeanor is the result of necessity. You have credited me with possessing an uncomplaining spirit. I do try to be firm, but my fate is hard. I have tried to fit myself for the future by hard study, and I feel within me the working of forces which I am sure would enable me to wring victory out of defeat. What my future will be I know not, but what my fate would have been were it not for the favorable conditions existing here I know full well—insanity. . . .

I am not afraid to look back to the tragic period in my life, but when I try to define and shape the unhappy event it assumes the form of a horrible, maddening dream, and I feel that I must have been insane. When I picture the faces of those who are gone and seek an answer to my mental questionings, I find I experienced no condemnation at the time—two faces, with eyes gazing upon me, strangely pitiful, that is all. I have been moving among the shadows this morning. The past seems very near and yet so far away. While this letter may have in it the echo of bitterness, I know you will not misunderstand it. Eighteen years old and seven and a half years in prison!

Upon his review of Wesley's letter, Madden was struck by its eloquence. When Madden first arrived, Wesley had seemed an immature and uneducated child. Now he was able to express his understanding of what he had done, his deep regret, and his determination to atone for his crime. Madden believed that Wesley deserved the opportunity to present his appeal to the public.

Madden knew how the pardon process worked for convicted murderers: proof of rehabilitation was often disputed by those who remembered the crimes and the victims, and rational arguments did not always carry the day. Debates and final votes by the General Assembly in these cases were often widely publicized by the newspapers, and members of the legislature, although sensitive to the views of their constituents, could be swayed by their colleagues and by strong sentiment across the state.

Personal advocates could play an important role in persuasion. Wesley, however, didn't have the means to pay an attorney. What Wesley needed was public support from influential Iowans. Carl Snyder was an important ally and a persuasive voice for Wesley, but Snyder was far removed from Iowa and communication with him was sporadic.

In early January 1897, Warden Madden wrote to the editor of the *Anamosa Eureka* asking whether he would be willing to publish Wesley's letter. Since readers would know Snyder by reputation and would remember the infamous Wesley Elkins, it was sure to attract attention. Madden enclosed a personal note assuring the editor that the letter was authentic and expressing his belief that Wesley posed no threat to the public. He hoped, he said, that Wesley's case might attract the attention of a prominent man or woman in the state.

Wesley's letter appeared in the *Eureka* on January 28, 1897. An editorial comment noted that the author's "thoughtfulness and grace of expression, as well as beauty of penmanship and correctness of punctuation" were noteworthy, especially from the pen of a young man who hadn't enjoyed the benefits of a formal education. The editorial commended the substantive strength of the appeal and recommended that Wesley be released from prison.

A week later, Wesley's letter was reprinted in the *Mount Vernon Hawkeye*, a newspaper published in a town fifteen miles away. Appearing under the large headline "A PATHETIC LETTER," his determination and sorrow earned him the sympathy of many readers.

Some people sent letters to Wesley at Anamosa to express their support. Nathan Gist, a young boy living in Cedar Falls, heard about the case. When Nathan's father, a professor at Coe College, arranged to tour Anamosa with his son, Nathan asked questions and found out more about Wesley. Nathan wrote to him, and the two began to correspond. Wesley told Nathan that he was grateful for any contact with people outside the prison.

Alida Griswold, from Perry, Iowa, often wrote to Wesley and sent him copies of books she recommended. As so many others, she was impressed with his maturity and expressiveness, and she wrote to Governor Drake to plead his case. She told the governor that "Wesley's letters prove that he is doing everything possible to educate himself even in that living tomb."

Cora, Wesley's older half-sister, also exchanged letters with Wesley. She was married and living in Minnesota at the time of the murders, and she hadn't seen her younger half-brother since he was seven years old. Unfortunately, none of the letters between the siblings, or between Wesley and other family members, exist in the archives. We do know, however, that Cora and Wesley were in close touch while he was in prison. As Wesley would say later, she was "as good and true a sister as a boy ever possessed," and she had promised that he would always have a home with her. She told him that, once he was free, she would bring him to Minnesota to join her family.

We don't know if Wesley corresponded with Mark, his older half-brother. Since Mark spent most summers with Cora and her family, he surely heard about Wesley's educational progress and maturation. A few years later, Mark would say publicly that he favored a parole for his brother.

Most significantly, though, it was James Harlan, a professor and administrator at Cornell College in Mount Vernon, who saw Wesley's letter in the local newspaper. Professor Harlan, who was known and respected throughout the state of Iowa, would become Wesley's most influential and important supporter.

In 1897, Harlan was fifty-one years old and at the mid-point of his career. He had been born in Ohio and moved to Iowa when he was a young boy, entering Cornell as a student in 1863. Shortly after his eighteenth birthday, he dropped out of college to join the Union Army, earning praise for his bravery on the battlefield. At the conclusion of the Civil War, he returned to Cornell, graduating in 1869 and marrying a classmate. After a four-year stint as superintendent of public schools in Cedar Rapids, Harlan accepted the new position of alumni professor at Cornell, teaching courses in Mathematics and Astronomy. In 1874, Harlan purchased land on the edge of campus and built a large two-story Victorian house where he and his wife, Janette, would live for nearly sixty years.

In his first years at the college, Harlan devoted most of his time to the classroom and his students, and he was highly regarded as a teacher. His intellectual interests ranged outside the classes he taught, and he was particularly fascinated by the emerging fields of ethics and psychology. By 1881, he had taken on administrative work, serving as vice president of the college, an office he was to hold for twenty-seven years, until 1908, when he was chosen as president of the college.

Reserved and modest in manner, Harlan was known to be exceedingly cautious in making decisions. According to a colleague, his approach "revealed that fine balance of intellect that is characteristic of the true scientist, weighing both sides of the question carefully and then coming to a conclusion only after marshaling all the facts involved."

As the top disciplinary authority at the college, Harlan became experienced in dealing with students, and he developed an absorbing interest in the moral and spiritual development of young people. Without children of his own, he focused on his influence over youth in the wider community, and he sought to live as a model to them, emphasizing the importance of education and displaying the personal virtues of fairness, generosity, and loyalty. In photographs from this period, he appears solemn and plain-featured, with a receding hairline and wire-rimmed glasses.

When Professor Harlan read Wesley's letter in the newspaper, he recalled the sensation the crime had provoked in the summer of 1889. The boy was now a young man, about the age of some of Harlan's students, and the professor was deeply moved by the boy's determination and expressiveness. Harlan was fascinated on an abstract level, considering how the case might prove that an individual could be transformed by reading, education, a safe environment, and positive role models. In his typical methodical fashion, Harlan began to solicit information and investigate the facts.

Harlan wrote to Carl Snyder first, asking for his help in contacting citizens of Clayton County, clergymen, and prison officials. Snyder forwarded reports he had collected, and they were not favorable. S. T. Richards, a prominent attorney in Clayton County, wrote about visiting the Elkins home a few hours after the murder. He described the crime scene in vivid detail and repeated the rumors that Wesley had inherited his "murderous disposition" from his birthmother, Matilda, who had plotted to kill her husband while she was pregnant with Wesley. A minister from Clayton County, unnamed in the newspaper, penned a letter agreeing with Richards' conclusion and stating that Wesley was "coldly, cruelly, maliciously vindictive." He expressed surprise that Professor Harlan was taking an interest in the case and wrote: "The pardon of Wesley Elkins would mean turning loose upon the world a person who has manifested a tremendous, innate (not acquired) capacity for crime. We have had enough 'degenerates' loose in the country, murdering by the wholesale. Society is to be considered as well as the individual."

Professor Harlan was skeptical about the idea of inherited criminality, and he was encouraged by the positive reports collected by Snyder from the current and former wardens at Anamosa. Warden Barr explained his conclusion that Wesley had been driven to commit his crime by mistreatment from his parents. He was joined by Warden Madden who thought Wesley was too young to have formed a criminal intent. Wardens Barr and Madden both described Wesley's remarkable educational progress and excellent behavior in glowing terms. The penitentiary far exceeded capacity, and so, more than ever, it seemed sensible to release those convicts like Wesley, who could be trusted to rejoin society. Barr and Madden agreed that Wesley was an exemplar of institutional success and deserved his chance at freedom. Warden Barr noted that "[T]he state cannot afford to punish for revenge, and society ought to be willing to quit when it is evident that further punishment can do no more good, especially when it is evident that no one will be injured by the release of a prisoner."

Harlan traveled to Anamosa to visit Wesley and was greatly impressed by the young man's personal demeanor and his intelligence. As Harlan would say later, he was convinced right away that Wesley was "possessed of really brilliant mental equipment." After that first visit, Harlan made up his mind to help Wesley, and for the next decade, Harlan devoted himself to that cause. Although his interest was initially triggered by theoretical issues, Harlan developed a personal and paternal bond with Wesley over the years. For his part, Wesley overcame his natural reticence, and he came to trust and confide in Professor Harlan.

15.

IN AUGUST 1897, Governor Francis Drake chose not to run for another term. As its nominee, the Republican Party chose Leslie Mortimer Shaw, a businessman largely unknown in the state.

Shaw had attended Cornell College and graduated in 1874. After college, Shaw had pursued a career as a lawyer and then as a banker. He was a serious man, self-confident, thoughtful, and a good public speaker. In the fall of 1897, he was elected by a large majority as Iowa's seventeenth governor. He was forty-nine years old and had ambitions for higher office. After four years as governor, he would join the cabinet of Theodore Roosevelt as Secretary of the Treasury, and in 1908, Shaw would run for the Republican nomination for president.

Shaw had graduated from Cornell when Professor Harlan was new to the faculty, and the two men had kept in contact since then, cultivating a friendship. Harlan was pleased by the election results, believing that it was a positive turn of events for Wesley. If Governor Drake forwarded Wesley's application to the 27th General Assembly in November 1897, Shaw would be in office the next spring, and he would be empowered to release Wesley Elkins from Anamosa.

In November 1897, Wesley filed his second appeal, this one addressed to Governor Drake. This time, he adopted Snyder's argument and wrote that he was too young at eleven years of age to have comprehended what he had done. He also expressed remorse for his crime:

> Were it possible to call the dead back again, I would gladly
> give my life for the privilege of doing so. But such a privilege is

denied me, and I can only say I feel regret, most bitter regret. I hope for the time when I may atone in part for my great wrong, by doing some good in the world. I feel that I am capable of taking care of myself; and that the sentiment of the mass of the thinking people of Iowa would favor my release. You are about to leave office and I hope that your last message will be marked by an act of mercy. . . . Appealing to the sympathy of the man, rather than to the executive,

    Yours most respectfully,

    Wesley Elkins

Governor Drake was reluctant to reject Wesley's appeal, and he included his application with several others he forwarded to the General Assembly. Following the requirements of the statute, the governor asked the *Iowa State Register* and the *Elkader Argus*, a Clayton County newspaper, to publish the required notices alerting the public to Wesley's request.

AT THE TIME Wesley was composing his application, the administration at the Anamosa State Penitentiary was in turmoil. Although Warden Madden was popular with the prisoners, his administration had been plagued with problems from the beginning. His clerk, W. C. Gilbreath, was accused of padding the payrolls, and after an investigation, was forced to resign. Madden himself was often criticized in the newspapers for his mismanagement and slack discipline. He was also guilty of nepotism: he had hired his oldest son, Charles, as deputy warden, and three other family members—another son, his brother-in-law, and a nephew—as prison guards.

Several specific incidents were cited as examples of Madden's poor judgment and permissiveness: he had accepted a watch as a gift from convicts, encouraged their participation in raffles and baseball games, and used profanity in their presence. A reporter who toured the prison noted that some cells "were decorated with pictures of every kind and description, chief among which are the photographs of half-naked actresses which are given away as prizes by cigarette manufacturing concerns." The notorious Rainsbarger brothers—serving life sentences for murder—had a dozen cages of singing canaries in their living quarters. Charles Curtis, who had secured opium from prison staff in the past, was a favorite of the guards and received special privileges. The reporter described a group of prisoners chatting with the guard on duty in the dining room:

> Each of the men wore his hair in the most fashionable style, cut, parted, and brushed as neatly as the swellest dude on Fifth Avenue. Curtis, the recently convicted bigamist, was among the number, and when he had tired of the conversation, he went to the other end of the room to play with some little Maltese kittens.

Most damning was the fact that during Madden's tenure, twenty-nine prisoners had escaped from the institution, and thirteen had never been recaptured. Madden's opponents strongly urged that a new warden be appointed.

SOON AFTER Wesley's application appeared in their local newspaper in November 1897, people in Clayton County reacted as they had two years earlier: they were angry and bitterly opposed, and they sought to make their voices heard. Petitions opposing Wesley's pardon were circulated throughout Clayton and adjoining counties, gathering more than 1,300 signatures by the time they were presented to the legislature that spring.

Hiram C. Bishop, editor and publisher of the *Clayton County Democrat*, was especially outspoken in his objections. Known as a man of strong convictions and dominating personality, Bishop was active in the Democratic Party and wielded considerable influence in Clayton County.

Bishop wrote several editorials for his newspaper in early January 1898, condemning Wesley and arguing against his release. Bishop had served as Clayton County's Superintendent of Schools before starting the *Democrat* in 1893, and he claimed to remember Wesley: "an unusually bright and attractive lad . . . but if you looked closely, you could see a peculiar expression in his steel-like eyes," indicating that he was "born with murder in his heart." The boy possessed "a morbid, beastly nature which in all probability he can never overcome this side of the grave." Bishop wrote:

> All sympathize with him and would freely throw the mantle of charity over his blood-stained life—forgive but not forget—yet they have no faith in his ability to keep in subjection his carnal nature.

Four days later, William Robert Boyd, editor of the *Cedar Rapids Republican*, echoed those views in his newspaper. Boyd, thirty-eight years old, was well respected in the state and had been the editor of the *Republican* for five years. To make the case against Wesley's release, Boyd repeated statements by the anonymous Clayton County citizen who had been interviewed two years earlier. That source, Boyd disclosed, was former Judge James Crosby, the lawyer who had acted as Wesley's defense counsel, and who was convinced that the boy had no moral conscience. The statements from Crosby had convinced Boyd that Wesley could not be rehabilitated.

The day after his editorial was published, Boyd received a letter from Professor Harlan, a man he respected as a leading educator. Professor Harlan suggested that Boyd had reached his conclusion without sufficient research and asked him to review a collection of materials, including letters Wesley had addressed to Harlan and to Carl Snyder. When Harlan extended an invitation for Boyd to come to the penitentiary to meet Wesley in person, Boyd agreed to go.

At the prison, the two men were greeted by Warden Madden, who led them to the library. Wesley was waiting there, standing at a window and gazing into the yard. Boyd later recalled his first impression: "As he came forward at the call of the warden to meet us, we saw a slight but compactly-built youth, easy in his bearing though somewhat diffident when presented. . . . He has a good forehead, deep-set eyes that do not shrink from your gaze, even though it be searching. The pallor characteristic of prisoners was present in a marked degree."

As Boyd conversed with Wesley, he noted that the young man was much as Harlan had described: he seemed remarkably mature and well-spoken. Despite that impression, though, Boyd had doubts that the letters signed by Wesley were authentic. It was well known that Charles Curtis, the bigamist and former newspaper man, was at Anamosa, and there were rumors that Curtis, rather than Wesley, must be the author. With Harlan's approval, Boyd conducted an experiment. He gave Wesley paper and pen and watched him compose a letter addressed to the General Assembly pleading his case for release. The several pages Wesley handed to him exhibited the same perfect punctuation and elegant diction that characterized the other letters he had signed.

On January 23, 1898, eight days after Boyd had expressed his strong opposition to Wesley's release, the Sunday issue of the *Republican* devoted the entire front page—seven columns across—to the case. A bold headline asked the question "SHOULD WESLEY ELKINS BE GRANTED A PARDON?" In slightly smaller type, the paper suggested the answer: "Earnest Students of the Remarkable Case Have Concluded that Society Will Not Be Endangered If the Pardon Prayed for Be Granted."

Although the editor had decided to support Wesley's release, Boyd began the feature with the two letters to Carl Snyder opposing the pardon. Readers learned the detailed story of the crime from S. T. Richards, the lawyer in Clayton County, who supported the theory that Wesley had inherited his murderous disposition from his mother. An unnamed minister characterized Wesley as "utterly destitute of moral faculty," and repeated the gossip that Wesley had declared that there were other people he wanted to kill.

The front page of the Republican followed the reports from Clayton County with four lengthy letters from Wesley, never before published. Two were addressed to the editor of the *Republican*, including the one written a few days earlier while Boyd watched, and two were written in 1897: one to Professor Harlan and one to the General Assembly.

In one of the letters to the editor, Wesley responded to the denunciation of him from James Crosby, his defense counsel, who had reached his conclusion about Wesley's degeneracy based only on brief conversations with an eleven-year-old child. Wesley wrote:

> Now is it reasonable to suppose that a boy so young would be capable of understanding the tenor of his own words? Is it not barely possible that Judge Crosby had a theory that I was a degenerate and questioned me along a line that would bring my answers into harmony with his belief?

Wesley made his case most powerfully in his letter to the General Assembly. He did not cite legal precedent, although he noted his young age at the time of the crime and his inability to comprehend the consequences. His lengthy appeal to the legislature was personal and emotional, repeating what he had been told by Warden Barr, and the hope that had sustained him for eight years.

> Some possibly will oppose me on the ground that my crime was most terrible. . . . Words cannot express the regret I feel, but can regret or imprisonment recall the dead? I would gladly give my life if I could recall them. But that I cannot do. What can I do?. . . .
> In the long years I have spent in this prison I have stood alone. I have carried a weight of prejudice that at times was almost too heavy to bear, yet notwithstanding all this I was buoyed up by hope. I felt that the time would come when justice would impel men to set aside the sentence in my case.

With hope of liberty as an incentive, I have struggled alone and unaided to develop and cultivate my mind, so as to fit myself to fill the position of a man among men. . . .

I am impelled to ask this question: Would you, if your child had offended and been punished, continue the punishment of that child after repentance had come, no matter what the child had done?. . . .

If I am released, I intend to work my way through college. I have a sister, as good and true a sister as a boy ever possessed in Lansing, Minn., and it is her wish that I should make my home with her. After I am released, I shall not expect any further help from anyone, nor will I ask it. . . .

I committed a terrible crime, that I know, but has not my punishment been severe—to spend my boyhood behind prison walls? I was but 11 years of age, I ask you especially to remember this. Could you take enough interest in me to look up my case and examine my prison record, and if you are satisfied, set aside the sentence in my case? You will not regret your kindness to a boy who finds himself almost alone in the world, with a fate worse than death staring him in the face.

I cannot tell you what it would mean to me. It was so long ago that I came here I can hardly remember what it was to be free. I was so little when I was put here, and I have never known what it was to be a boy like other boys. Now I am a young man, determined to make a success in life; and I am sure if you have confidence in me I will not abuse it.

I ask you to think what it means to grow up in a prison, to feel that you might be out in the world making your own way—or, at least, to struggle to do your best—and to then realize that you are shut up here—for life! Sometimes, thinking about it, I feel as if I would go mad. I do not know that anyone else can understand what it means.

I make this appeal to your sense of justice. I appeal to your humanity to give me another chance to begin anew my unhappy life. Will you help me?

The *Republican* added a final comment at the end of the page in support of Wesley's release. The note acknowledged that some believed that a child could be "cursed before his birth" and doomed by his heredity to a life of crime. But the alternative theory seemed more likely: that the character of a young child was subject to change, and moral consciousness could develop with proper environmental and social influences. Thus, even a child subject to negative prenatal influences and who had done wrong at an early age could develop in a positive direction under the right conditions, learning self-control and abiding by moral principles. Wesley Elkins seemed such a case.

Admittedly, many people had doubts about giving Wesley a full pardon. The *Republican* suggested another option to ease their fears. Offenders guilty of less serious crimes were often granted conditional releases, so why not do the same for Wesley? Make him prove that he is trustworthy by requiring that he obey certain strict rules: he would have to live under the charge of a responsible guardian and demonstrate respect for the law. Satisfactory completion of the probationary period would end with a full and complete pardon, while misconduct would result in his immediate return to Anamosa for the rest of his life. Society could be protected from harm, and Wesley given a second chance to live outside the prison walls.

Soon after the article in the *Republican* came out, others wrote letters in support of Wesley's appeal. One was from the Matron at Anamosa, Mrs. Jennie Powers, who had watched Wesley in prison. Writing on official Anamosa letterhead, she recommended him as an excellent candidate for release, remarking on "his love of study [and] his remarkable thirst for knowledge and a mind capable of digesting heavy subjects." Another came from Reverend A. B. Curran, a pastor of the M. E. Church in Quasqueton, Iowa, who had lived two miles from the Elkins when he was a boy. Curran had known John and Hattie Elkins, and he wrote that "I feel justified in saying that the boy was greatly abused and really driven to commit the crime." Wesley's continued imprisonment, according to Curran, was "a great injustice and an unchristian act."

Professor Harlan continued to be Wesley's strongest advocate, always emphasizing the evidence that Wesley was rehabilitated. Harlan solicited additional testimonials from Anamosa officials, and he traveled to Des Moines to talk to individual legislators, promising that he would be happy to accept responsibility for Wesley if he were released.

Senator John Everall from Clayton County was the leading voice against Wesley Elkins in the General Assembly. A descendant of one of the original pioneer families from the county, the senator was considered a man of integrity and judgment. He had served the county in many roles: as teacher, school superintendent, auditor, and since 1892 as a member of the General Assembly. He was respected by his colleagues and trusted by his constituents. Senator Everall did not hesitate to argue against Elkins on behalf of those he represented, and he publicly pledged at an early stage that he would do everything in his power to keep Elkins in prison.

At Anamosa, Wesley received a steady stream of visitors throughout the spring. Members of the Committees on Pardons interviewed him, and other legislators traveled to the prison on their own. Two ministers from Clayton County, initially against the pardon, changed their opinions after their trip to Anamosa. Senator Everall was also affected by his conversation with Wesley. After a two-hour interview, Everall admitted that his feelings had softened, and that he was not forever set against the pardon. If, at some point in the future, he could be convinced that Wesley was not a danger to others, he was "quite ready to be charitable."

Sentiment among legislators was divided. Supporters expressed optimism, but they recognized the bitter opposition and feared that a defeat would prejudice Wesley's chances in the future. Senator William Mitchell, who was a good friend of Harlan's, proposed a solution that he hoped would satisfy both sides. Considering the strong opposition, he suggested that supporters would persuade

Wesley to withdraw his application if they had assurance that it would be considered by the next General Assembly in two years. Senator Everall was amenable to the agreement, but he couldn't guarantee that his constituents would change their minds. Wesley's supporters could not have known then that Senator Everall would no longer be in office for the next debate over Wesley's pardon, and that he would be replaced by Hiram Bishop, one of Wesley's most impassioned opponents in Clayton County.

The two sides struck the deal in late March 1898. Professor Harlan knew that Wesley would be keenly disappointed, but Harlan assured him that release would come in two years. Harlan trusted that the General Assembly would forward a favorable recommendation to Governor Shaw, who would, in turn, sign the pardon papers. In late March, the *Cedar Rapids Republican* reported that the petition would be withdrawn and that legislators had "tacitly agreed" to approve Wesley's pardon in 1900.

In gratitude, Wesley composed a letter of appreciation. He sent it to Boyd and asked that it be published in his newspaper. Wesley offered sincere thanks to his friends for their kindness and unswerving support and expressed his great hope of entering college in the future so as to "lay the foundation for a true and industrious manhood." He understood that the pressure from Clayton County was great and could only hope that time would soften the feelings of those against him.

A FEW WEEKS LATER, the General Assembly recommended conditional pardons for two murderers: James Johnson and Bernard Kennedy. Governor Shaw approved and signed the papers on April 12, 1898.

Johnson had been incarcerated at Fort Madison since January 1885 for shooting and killing his brother. Kennedy had served ten years at Anamosa after being convicted of killing his wife and mutilating her body. He steadfastly maintained his innocence throughout his trial and imprisonment. Kennedy's case attracted more attention than Johnson's, with supporters in the legislature arguing that the critical testimony of Kennedy's two young children, who had not seen the crime committed, was unreliable and uncorroborated.

In a deviation from tradition, these men were paroled instead of pardoned. To remain free, they were required to satisfy conditions, including abstaining from alcohol, avoiding establishments where intoxicating liquor was sold or consumed, and living as law-abiding citizens.

16.

ON APRIL 1, 1898, William Hunter, a fifty-three-year-old resident of Belle Plaine, Iowa, became the fifth man to assume the position of warden and chief administrator of Anamosa Penitentiary, replacing Philander Madden. Unlike his predecessors who had served as county sheriffs, Hunter had no experience in law enforcement. A native Iowan, Hunter had joined the Union Army as a drummer boy when he was sixteen, participating in the Battle of Shiloh. He was well-educated, with a degree from Grinnell College, and had served two terms as the postmaster of Belle Plaine, Iowa.

On Friday, June 17, 1898, Warden Hunter hosted a delegation of nearly fifty community leaders. The group included local ministers, attorneys, businessmen, judges, and State Senator Frederick Ellison. The new warden used the occasion to introduce his new administration to the public and to emphasize the progress that had been made since the fire.

Hunter explained with pride that the penitentiary had recently adopted the Bertillon system to classify incoming prisoners based on their physical characteristics. The technique had been used in American prisons since 1887. Developed before the modern use of fingerprinting, the system was the brainchild of a Frenchman, Alphonse Bertillon, to provide permanent identification of convicts. Scars, tattoos, hair and eye color, and other easily detectable physical markings were noted, along with precise measurements of the prisoner's height, torso, right ear, left foot, forearm, and skull. The dimensions of the skull were particularly important since researchers in the new field of Phrenology theorized that the

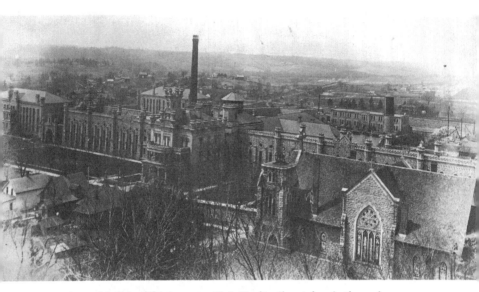

An aerial view of the Anamosa State Penitentiary taken in the early 1900s.
(Courtesy of Steve Wendl and the Anamosa State Penitentiary Prison
History website.)

size and shape of a person's skull provided clear evidence of criminal tendencies and incorrigibility. To obtain the information, the
prisoner was required to sit without moving while a staff member
used a crude vice-like tool to measure his head from crown to
forehead and from temple to temple.

The warden also reported on a new grading system established
as an incentive for good behavior. Convicts would be assigned
to one of three grades based on their records of conduct, and
members of each grade would be clothed so they could be identified: first grade in gray suits; second grade in plaid suits; third
grade—the incorrigibles—in stripes. First and second grade prisoners would have separate dining halls, while third grade would
be confined to eat in their cells.

After these introductory remarks, Hunter took the group on a
two-hour tour, pointing out areas of new construction: cells for

prisoners, sleeping quarters for guards, a new system of showers with temperature controls for the bathers, and a woodworking shop where prisoners would construct frames for doors and windows. He was particularly proud of the rebuilt library. Although the fire in August had destroyed most of the collection, close to 5000 books had been donated or purchased since then, and would soon fill the shelves. The library was on the second floor, next to a room with a new printing press for the penitentiary's use.

IN 1898, Charles Curtis, the bigamist, was working in the kitchen, where, as he put it, he "took up the bread-knife and started in to slaughter the staff of life." In the summer of 1898, Warden Hunter gave him a new assignment more in line with his experience as a publisher: he was to inventory the books for the new library, and when that task was completed, Curtis was to write and publish a prison newspaper.

Curtis was happy to accept the position, which was a promotion of sorts. Warden Hunter assigned Wesley Elkins to assist him. The two men worked together to catalog the books, with Curtis taking time out to make a list of one thousand additional titles that he hoped the library would procure. Curtis then turned his attention to the newspaper, while Wesley, now with the title of librarian, was given full responsibility for cataloging, shelving, and distributing the books.

The first issue of the *Anamosa Prison Press* appeared on Saturday, July 30, 1898. The paper was an eight-page, three-column paper, printed on the newly acquired press and distributed throughout the penitentiary. Copies were also available to the public, and Curtis later reported, in what was surely an exaggeration, that "it became within a few weeks one of the most widely quoted papers in the country."

Charles Curtis and Wesley Elkins made an odd couple—the bigamist with literary skills and an outgoing personality, and the quiet, studious young man—and their crimes and backgrounds were vastly different. Their shared interests in books and in good writing brought them closer, and Wesley no doubt learned a good deal from Curtis during the hours they spent together. Curtis noted his association with Wesley in his memoir, and when Curtis gained his freedom in September 1899, he handed over the editorship of the *Prison Press* to Wesley.

One of the last issues Curtis edited was published on Memorial Day 1899. It featured photos and profiles of the guards and other prison personnel who had served in the military. The issue contained regular columns, such as "Local Prison Chat" and "The Prison Chapel" by Chaplain E. G. Beyer. One news article noted that crime in Iowa was decreasing, but hospitalizations for insanity were on the rise.

Although the *Prison Press* continued to be published for many decades, future editions lacked much of the flair of the issues edited by Curtis.

THE NEXT eighteen months passed quietly for prisoners at Anamosa. Warden Hunter continued to make some changes in the routines, and he oversaw physical improvements, but there were no major incidents. That was not the case, however, at the state reform school for girls in Mitchellville, Iowa.

The reform school was home to 186 girls, and in late October 1899, the young women rioted. More than seventy of them actively participated in the rebellion. The revolt captured the attention of Iowans, with newspapers featuring vivid details on their front pages.

The disturbance began at dinner on Sunday evening, October 22. Although the girls never clearly articulated their grievances, later investigations by the state showed that a new administration had put inexperienced staff members in charge. Rules were not consistently applied, and severe punishments—including spanking girls with rubber tubes—were inflicted for minor infractions.

The ringleader was a sixteen-year-old girl named Maude Jeffries.

After instigating the outbreak, she and several others had tried to set fires in their dormitory. Over the course of several hours, the girls rampaged through the buildings and across the grounds, shouting obscenities at the officials who tried to quell the uprising. The rioters used butcher knives, kitchen utensils, and scissors—recently purchased for the required sewing classes—as weapons, and threw pieces of furniture, lamps, and washbowls. When the superintendent could not regain control, he sent pleas for help to the town. More than thirty men arrived, and some of them were seriously injured as they fought to restore order.

Chaos reigned. The girls smashed everything that was breakable: windows, mirrors, light bulbs, ceramic pitchers, and slop jars. The dormitory halls and the kitchen area were filled with shattered glass and broken pottery. The girls drank fermented fruit juice found in the cellar. Some played the piano and danced and sang, while others stood outside the building, attacking anyone who came close. Several girls rode away on bicycles they stole from the villagers. Damages to the building were later estimated to be at least $10,000.

It took more than twenty-four hours and help from Sheriff Jim Stout and his deputies to quell the riot. Girls were dragged from the building, handcuffed, and locked in the basement until they could be transported to the jail in Des Moines. In the days that followed, they hardly seemed contrite. An article in the *Des Moines Daily Capital* included a quote from Maude Jeffries: "Oh, we had a hell of a time and I guess we tore things loose. We smashed up everything and I fought with the officers and had a good time."

Many reporters who covered the story were quick to label the girls as dangerous criminals. There were reports that the girls had attacked the men not only with weapons but also with their teeth, proving that they were vicious and unnatural. They were characterized as incorrigible and without the potential for rehabilitation, "poisonous influences" on the more innocent girls who could still be trained in womanly ways.

Other reporters were more charitable and sought to understand why the girls had behaved as they did. They discovered scandalous conditions at the institution, where girls were often punished for minor rule violations by whippings and long solitary confinements. They were mistreated by male staff members, who often made lewd comments and watched while the girls bathed. Given the treatment the girls endured, the reporters were not surprised that they had rebelled.

Susan Glaspell, a young reporter who visited the girls in jail, was among those hesitant to label them as depraved and unnatural. Although they were brash and outspoken, she found that they were much like other girls their age. She noted the pleasure they took in singing a song for her, and she watched as they responded to a baby with affection and delight. Perhaps, Glaspell thought, they were not innately bad, despite the savagery and violence they had displayed. In a column written for the *Des Moines Daily News*, Glaspell noted their sad backgrounds: most had lived in poverty and without parents or a home. Were the girls naturally depraved? Or were they the products of their unfortunate childhoods, growing up without love, guidance, or protection? If that were the case, perhaps the girls could still be saved.

Susan Glaspell would not forget the questions she had raised in her column about Mitchellville, and they were in the forefront of her mind when she followed the controversy surrounding Wesley's pardon in the next several years. In 1903, she would publish a short story entitled "In the Face of His Constituents" that was inspired by Wesley's case. Again, she would suggest that a child's behavior could not be entirely blamed on immutable character flaws.

17.

IN NOVEMBER 1899, a few weeks after the Mitchellville riot, Wesley Elkins filed his third appeal. Wesley asked Governor Shaw "most earnestly and respectfully" to present his application to the Twenty-Eighth General Assembly for its investigation and advice. Having continued his record of exemplary behavior, Wesley had good reason to feel optimistic.

Interest in Wesley's case and support for his release had been building in the two years since he had last applied to the governor for pardon. In June 1899, E. Wade Koons, a junior at Coe College in Cedar Rapids and the son of a Presbyterian minister, had won the college essay contest by presenting an impassioned and well-argued essay about Wesley's crime and pleas for freedom. The essay contained many of the arguments made on Wesley's behalf by his numerous supporters. Koons recounted the facts of the crime, then focused on Wesley's home life and young age, stating that Wesley had been beaten and abused and treated as "a beast of burden." Noting that Wesley was too young at the time of the murders to have developed a mature sense of right and wrong, Koons went on to argue that life at Anamosa had allowed him the opportunity for moral development and education. In conclusion, Koons asserted, "In the place of the degenerate who entered the penitentiary at Anamosa ten years ago, stands today a man with a man's abilities and a man's conscience, ready and eager to take a man's place in the toil and strife of the world."

After Koons read his essay aloud to a packed crowd in the college auditorium, the judges declared him the winner of the Dows

Prize. Six months later, in December 1899, the essay was printed in the *Coe College Courier* where it received more public attention.

When Governor Shaw received Wesley's application in November, he had just been reelected as governor, easily winning a second term. Although Republicans remained firmly in control of the legislature, Shaw knew that he would face a difficult political struggle in the two years ahead. The Republican party was deeply divided between conservatives and progressives, and the conflicts between the two sides had grown increasingly bitter. Shaw was closely aligned with conservatives—they had put him forth as their nominee for governor two years earlier—but he was anxious to remain friendly with the progressive wing. In order to achieve his goal of higher office, he would need broad and unified Republican support.

The question of Wesley's pardon would provoke heated debate, and Clayton County citizens were sure to mount a furious campaign against him. Senator Everall, leader of the opposition in 1898, had expressed a willingness to reconsider his position, but he was no longer in the Senate. Hiram Bishop, the editor of the *Clayton County Democrat* and one of the loudest voices opposing Wesley's release, had taken his place. His constituents were confident that Senator Bishop would represent them with blistering attacks on Wesley and on those who supported his pardon.

Governor Shaw was eager to avoid controversy so early in his second term, and there were other reasons that made him reluctant to move forward with Wesley's case. Although he knew and respected Professor Harlan, Shaw had been alarmed by Bishop's warning in 1898 that a moral degenerate could infect the populace if he was allowed to multiply. Robert Quigley, the county attorney who had prosecuted Wesley for murder, had also written to Shaw in 1898. Quigley described his impressions after interviewing Wesley:

> I concluded that Wesley was made of the same material but of sterner stuff than the James Brothers. . . . [H]is moral nature is

of the coldest steel [and] he never can realize the impact of his acts and should not be turned out to beget more of his kind and through slight provocation destroy other lives. He will not be so easily caught another time.

Governor Shaw made his decision. Although he asked the General Assembly to discuss four appeals, Wesley's application remained on his desk.

Shaw wrote directly to Professor Harlan, explaining that he believed that Wesley was "so constituted mentally as to be measurably irresponsible" and afflicted with "abnormal proclivities that [he is] incapable of controlling." Accordingly, Shaw wrote, "If the General Assembly were to authorize his pardon, I should be compelled to decline it; and this being true, I ought not to put the state to the expense of an investigation."

Harlan tried to persuade Shaw to change his mind. He traveled to Des Moines to meet with him in person, reminding him that legislators in the previous session had promised to recommend Wesley for pardon. Shaw stood firm. He would not reconsider, although he agreed to offer some small consolation to Wesley: if he received an application from Wesley in November 1901, he would forward it to the Twenty-Ninth General Assembly for discussion. Shaw did not plan to run for governor again, so he would not be in office in the spring of 1902. If the legislature were to recommend Wesley's pardon, his successor would be the one to make the final decision.

As Wesley would learn that spring, only two convicted murderers—Cornelius Moelcher and Thomas Kelly—were granted their freedom in 1900. Moelcher, a German immigrant, had been convicted of killing his uncle thirty years earlier. He couldn't speak English at that time, and supporters argued that he hadn't received adequate legal counsel. After discussion, most of the legislators voted to recommend him for pardon, but Governor Shaw chose to parole Moelcher. He would be pardoned after ten years only if he obeyed stated rules, including abstaining from liquor, remaining employed, and reporting to the governor once a month.

The decision to parole rather than to pardon a prisoner had been accepted in other states, but it was still controversial in Iowa. Some argued that the willingness to grant conditional releases would result in too many dangerous criminals back on the streets. Others applauded the change, noting that the possibility of a return to prison would be an incentive for good behavior.

William Boyd, the editor of the *Cedar Rapids Republican*, supported the decision to parole rather than to pardon. When he wrote about Wesley's case in 1898, he had suggested that Wesley should be paroled first and then pardoned only if he satisfied certain conditions. If he failed, he would be back behind bars.

Governor Shaw issued a full pardon to only one man in the spring of 1900. Thomas Kelly had been convicted of first-degree murder and sentenced to life at Anamosa when he was seventy-two years old. Kelly had served twelve years when the legislators discussed his case in the spring of 1900. He argued that his conviction was unjust; his wife, who was involved in the crime, had only been found guilty of manslaughter. Kelly's appeal had been considered and rejected several times. Now he was eighty-four and in ill health, and this time, the pardon resolution passed with a unanimous vote. The papers were rushed to the governor to sign, and the news was flashed across the wires to Warden Hunter at Anamosa. Thirteen hours later, Kelly died in his bed at Anamosa.

For Wesley, Governor Shaw's decision to hold back his application meant another delay. It would be the fall of 1901 before he could submit his next appeal for freedom.

18.

IN EARLY SEPTEMBER 1901, two months before his appeal for pardon was due that November, Wesley Elkins collapsed outside the prison's dining hall. The *Anamosa Prison Press* reported:

> Just as the lines neared the Dining room door, Wednesday evening, going to supper, our librarian, 1900, reeled and fell in a faint. He was taken to the Hospital, where it was ascertained that the boy's nervous system is in a weak condition. Long and close confinement has had its effects on the boy. He has been librarian about seven years, and the close confinement that he has endured would have told on a much stronger man, although 1900 has done little complaining.

Wesley spent several days in the hospital. When he was discharged, he was transferred to the engine room, with the hope that a different environment among other men might be good for his spirits. The warden knew that Wesley was suffering from stress and anxiety as he waited to file his next bid for freedom in November.

At the beginning of the new century, political challenges and social change had dominated the news in Iowa. Women's suffrage was a topic of great debate, and many of its strongest proponents were influential in raising issues about children. The National Congress of Mothers, an organization formed to focus on child welfare, had held its annual meeting in Des Moines in 1900, and Iowa members created a state chapter soon after that. From its inception, the group worked hard throughout Iowa to publicize contemporary ideas about the importance of schooling and parental guidance in early development, and to propose new explanations for the serious problem of juvenile crime, emphasizing circumstances such as neglect, poverty, and negative influences at home. The notion that children should be treated differently under the law was gaining strong advocates, with supporters arguing that Iowa should follow the lead of Illinois, which had established the first juvenile court system in 1899. Iowa had reform schools for boys and girls established to house delinquents and offenders of minor crimes. By 1902, support in Iowa was growing for the establishment of a separate institution for young criminals, separating them from adults. Advocates for change stressed that children, still at an early stage of development, were most dramatically shaped by their environment and by those around them, and so offered the greatest promise of rehabilitation.

The increased public attention to children was a favorable trend for Wesley. The mistreatment he suffered as a child—now more widely known to the public—was seen as a mitigating factor. And his transformation into an articulate and intelligent young man who now pleaded for his release seemed to justify the belief held by reformers: that a child could develop a moral conscience with education and positive adult guidance.

The child-saving movement was influential in advocating that the age of the offender be considered as the most significant factor. As Wesley had discovered in 1895, common law supported that view, with courts recognizing a presumption that a child age fourteen or younger was incapable of acting with criminal intent. As progressive reformers grew more concerned about the increasing number of juvenile offenders, they cited theories of mental and emotional growth that were consistent with the legal rule.

At the same time, however, others were continuing to believe that inherited abnormalities explained crime. They accepted the idea that some people, those guilty of the most violent crimes, carried a mental defect that could be passed on through the generations. Eugenic thinking was in its early stages in 1902, but some, identifying themselves as criminal anthropologists, were spreading the idea that these offenders, if released and allowed to reproduce, could infect the population. Although these notions were later discredited, they had already stimulated forceful arguments against Wesley, and these would be repeated in the spring of 1902.

Iowa politics were tumultuous in 1901, characterized by bitter infighting within the controlling Republican Party. The progressives had been outraged when Shaw chose a conservative to replace a senator who had died in office in January 1900. With Shaw unwilling to run for a third term, they mobilized to nominate Alfred Cummins, a known progressive, to run for governor in November 1901.

Alfred Cummins was not a native Iowan. He had been born in Pennsylvania in 1850, moved to Iowa as a teenager, and then relocated to Illinois, starting a law practice in Chicago. Eventually, he returned to Iowa and settled in Des Moines, representing corporations and businessmen in the courtroom. Despite his success, Cummins wasn't content with his work; he wanted a bigger stage, a position of influence and visibility in state politics.

After a vigorous campaign throughout Iowa, speaking to enthusiastic audiences about the corrupting influence of special interests on state government, Cummins won the Republican primary in August. In November, Cummins was elected governor by an overwhelming majority. His victory reflected a significant change in the state's political climate, consistent with the trend toward progressivism throughout the country.

In late November, Wesley filed his fourth appeal for pardon, again addressed to Governor Shaw, who would leave office in January. Professor Harlan also wrote Governor Shaw, reminding him that he had promised to forward Wesley's request to the General Assembly. Despite his personal reservations, Shaw abided by his word, knowing that Cummins would be the one to make the final decision. Setting a record, Shaw asked the legislature to investigate all thirteen appeals he had received from murderers sentenced to life in prison, including Wesley's. It would be one of Shaw's last acts as Iowa's chief executive.

On January 16, 1902, Albert Cummins was inaugurated as the eighteenth governor of Iowa. Legislators arrived in Des Moines for the festivities and for the start of the Twenty-Ninth General Assembly. Throughout the spring, the legislative sessions continued to draw people to the city, coming from across the state to make their views known to their representatives.

In the early months of 1902, women were especially visible in the capital city, eager to advocate for causes that were of particular interest to them. The state chapter of the National Congress of Mothers gathered again in January. A month later, women crowded into the legislative galleries to hear the Senate debate the Women Suffrage Bill. Supporters celebrated victory after the vote in the Senate, only to be bitterly disappointed a month later, when the bill was defeated in the House. Newspapers vividly described the statehouse scene, with women filling the galleries, crowding into the cloak rooms, and then swarming into the corridors after the vote. One reporter called the demonstrations a stampede.

The pardon for Wesley would be considered in late March. Senator Hiram Bishop had already declared that Clayton County would stand firm in its opposition. Bishop, the county's former Superintendent of Schools, repeated his impression that Wesley had a violent disposition, and declared that nothing would change his mind. His constituents agreed with him. Most of them signed new petitions protesting Wesley's freedom.

In early January 1902, Wesley addressed a letter directly to "The Citizens of Clayton County," which was published in several Iowa newspapers. Expressing remorse for his past actions, Wesley pleaded with them to "thoroughly investigate my conduct, record, my present mental and moral condition, before taking any action adverse to my release." He described how education had changed him so that "the evil tendencies manifested in the boy had been permanently eradicated in the man." He begged the people of Clayton County to act with Christian charity and mercy and give him the chance to rejoin society. He would prove that he could "live in obedience to the law of the land, and in harmony with the law of God, and with the rightful claims of my fellow men."

Five weeks later, an editorial purported to respond to Wesley on behalf of the citizens of Clayton County. First published in the *Arlington News*—the newspaper in a small town in Fayette County, a few miles west of the Clayton County boundary—and then reprinted in the *Des Moines Daily Capital*, it warned Wesley that they would not be deceived by any letters published under his name. They suspected that "the bigamist editor Curtis" was in fact the author of those, and, in any case, only "sentimentalists" would be swayed by his educated words. Others remembered what he had done, how he had lied to them and gone about town "talking about the affair as if a couple of rabbits had been slain." People in Clayton County would not be fooled by Wesley Elkins now:

> If young Elkins is doing so well in the prisons, is studying so ardently, is so well demeanored and behaved and is making a man of himself at such rapid strides, it would be cruel to let him out and thereby subject him to the temptations and pitfalls of a wicked world and the liability of a downfall. He is young yet and the proper place for him is undoubtedly where he is in the prison.
>
> When these known desperadoes and murderers are once safely in the penitentiary what in the name of common sense is the use in taking chances by letting them out? Let them alone.

19.

WESLEY ELKINS ALWAYS refuted stories of his misbehavior while he was incarcerated, and wardens and guards consistently confirmed his exemplary conduct there. But he could not deny what he had done as a child. Only rarely did he talk about his parents, explain his acts, or defend himself. Instead, he focused on his age and immaturity at the time, and his mental and moral development since then.

These were, of course, the very points that Professor Harlan stressed, and he and other supporters were well organized this time to make the case on Wesley's behalf. Harlan visited the capitol early in the legislative session to meet with House and Senate members and give interviews to reporters. Newspapers reprinted letters from Wesley, including a new one addressed directly to the legislators. Wesley again pled for his release: "If my young life is ever to be turned into an avenue of usefulness ought it not to be now, while I am young and strong and hopeful of the future? Why not now before incentive to action is lacking and spirit of ambition departs, leaving behind a weary, hopeless wreck?"

The House and Senate Committees on Penitentiaries and Pardons moved forward separately with their investigations. Members of the committees interviewed Wesley at Anamosa, and they held joint sessions to hear from prison administrators and from Clayton County residents. They also considered the many letters they received, some vehemently opposed to Wesley's release, and others expressing their support.

On February 11, J. H. Haskins, a former resident of Clayton County, wrote directly to Senator William Whipple, the chairman of the Senate Committee on Penitentiaries and Pardons. Haskins had visited Wesley in prison, and he supported his release. He described Wesley as "a sadly neglected child" who had been physically abused. Haskins asked that the legislators take into account that Wesley was "born of a hard family, of bad parents."

The Reverend A. B. Curran, who had written a letter in 1898, wrote again, on February 25, 1902, to argue for a pardon. He had been a close friend of Wesley's older half-brother, Mark, and claimed to know the family well. According to Curran, Wesley's father had a quick temper, and Wesley's home life was "anything but congenial."

In addition to sharing his own observations of the Elkins family, Curran had solicited letters of support from three boys—now adults—who had known Wesley before the murders. Curran submitted the letters of Wesley's boyhood acquaintances along with his own to the Senate committee.

James Porter, son of the man who owned the house where the murders had taken place, described Wesley as an "average boy" and "well behaved." Others noted his young age and his quiet disposition, and one wrote that Wesley "was not a boy who would seek to pick a quarrel." All three of the letters urged the legislators to recommend Wesley for pardon.

Reverend Curran wrote again to add that both of Wesley's older half-siblings supported Wesley's release. Curran had heard directly from Mark, and Cora had repeated the offer she had made to Wesley in 1898: if he were released from prison, she would welcome him into her home in Minnesota to join her family. Cora and Mark were both children of John Elkins—the victim of the crime—and they had known Wesley since he was born. Cora had lived nearby her father when Wesley was a baby; she remembered when he was sent to Waterloo several years later, and then when the seven-year-old boy had been returned to his father's house. She had overlapped with Wesley for just a few months, until she married George Bassett and moved to Minnesota. Two years later, she had given birth to a son, naming him "Wesley" after her younger brother.

Supporters were surprised by the continuing intense opposition to Wesley's pardon that continued through the spring. Typically, those who were released had support from their communities, but that was not the case for Wesley. The lawyers who had prosecuted and defended Wesley and the judge who had sentenced him, believed that Wesley deserved to stay where he was. Clayton County residents resented being characterized as harsh and unforgiving when they were relying on knowledge that outsiders lacked. According to the *Elkader Argus*, "the thought of a pardon is repulsive to say the least."

In late March, a long article appeared in the *Des Moines Daily Leader,* expanding on the virulent protests coming from Clayton County. The arguments had been made before—that Wesley was a born criminal, whose degeneracy could not be cultivated out of him—but this time the stories about his mother that had circulated for years in Clayton County were reported to a wider audience. Wesley's crime was now more overtly blamed on heredity, and the idea of him as a carrier of criminality was made more explicit. According to the article, he was "born with the brand of Cain on his brow." The article went on: "The degeneracy of Wesley Elkins is firmly believed by the people of Clayton County to be a verification of the Mosaic prophecy that the sins of the fathers shall be visited upon the children, even unto the third and fourth generations."

Considering the intense opposition, supporters began to accept conditional release as the best solution, and a resolution recommending parole rather than pardon was drafted. Under the resolution, Wesley could be pardoned in ten years if he complied with the conditions. He would be required to stay with Professor Harlan until given permission otherwise, and he would be forbidden to enter Clayton County or any counties adjoining Clayton.

At last, Wesley's case came before the two legislative commit-

tees on pardons. Twelve other applications had already been discussed. Six prisoners had been rejected, and six had been recommended for conditional parole and would be debated on the
capitol floor.

Like Wesley, these men had been sentenced to life in prison
for first-degree murder. William Young was a bootblack who had
killed another man five years earlier in a dispute over a game of
dice, and legislators accepted Young's claim that he was only trying to quiet the violence that had erupted. George Stanley, sixty-
two years old, had been in prison since he was thirty; he had killed
a man in what he claimed was self-defense. Now, he was blind and
in poor health, and his family had offered to give him a home.
Theodore Bushwick had spent twenty-three years in Anamosa's
insane ward after killing his wife and father-in-law, and he was
said to be fully recovered. Joseph McCrary, in prison for twenty-
three years, had apparently been incited by others when he shot a
brutal boss. Otto Otten, said to be an ignorant and inexperienced
German boy, had been enticed by his employer's forty-two-year-
old wife to have sex with her and then kill her husband; Otten
had been in prison for twenty-four years and had acquired valuable skills as a stonecutter. Jack Ballew had been drunk when,
twenty years earlier, he had killed a gambler who threatened his
life. At Anamosa, he had become proficient as a photographer.
When Ballew's parole was granted, the *Prison Press* published an
editorial expressing regret that he would be leaving, starting with
the question "Who's going to get Jack's job?"

Wesley's appeal was sure to be the most controversial, and so
was saved for last. Talks among committee members went on behind closed doors, and when they finally voted, the resolution in
favor of Wesley's release was defeated in both committees. The
counts were close—in both cases only one vote decided the result—but it seemed that the question would again be resolved
without full debate on the capitol floor.

Wesley's supporters were unwilling to concede defeat. Senate Committee members on the losing side argued that Bishop had prejudged the case, and so his vote should not count. In the House Committee, supporters claimed that widespread public attention merited full discussion by all representatives. Opponents eventually agreed; the resolution would be introduced in both houses without recommendation, and minority reports would be permitted. When newspapers publicized the upcoming debate, they predicted that the case would inspire some of the most emotional speeches of the entire session.

The Senate convened on the morning of April 2, 1902, with the matter of Wesley's parole first on the agenda. The gallery was crowded with spectators who filled the seats and stood along the back walls of the chamber, and newspapers reported that most of them were in favor of Wesley.

That morning, legislators had found small pamphlets on their desks, featuring a photograph of Wesley on the front cover. It was the same image of Wesley as a young schoolboy that had enraged citizens of Clayton County when it first appeared in the *Elkader Register* in 1890 next to Wesley's confession.

The pamphlet had been created and distributed by Professor Harlan. Titled "WESLEY ELKINS: AN APPEAL AND STATEMENTS OF EX-WARDENS BARR AND MADDEN AND WARDEN HUNTER," the pamphlet contained four letters. The first was Wesley's letter addressed to the citizens of Clayton County, dated January 6, 1902, which had been previously published in the Des Moines newspapers. The other three letters had been solicited by Harlan from the wardens who had supervised Wesley during his years at Anamosa. Wardens Barr and Madden wrote at great length describing their initial impressions of Wesley and commenting on his growth and maturity. Warden Hunter's letter was the shortest and closed with this sentence: "He is quiet, industrious and respectful, and his record clear on the books of any infraction of the rules." All three wardens expressed their support for Wesley's parole.

Senator William Whipple, the forty-four-year-old chairman of the Committee on Pardons and a first-term senator rose from his seat to begin the proceedings. Whipple was a distinguished-looking man with a round face, receding hairline and a thick mustache. A graduate of the Iowa College of Law, he had practiced law in his hometown of Vinton, Iowa, for more than two decades before entering politics. He was experienced in the courtroom and was known to be a persuasive advocate.

Whipple introduced the minority report from the committee in favor of the parole and read aloud the conditions that would be required of Wesley: avoiding evil associations, obeying the laws, and abstaining from intoxicating liquors for ten years. Violation of any of the terms would send him back to prison. If Wesley complied, he would be granted a full pardon at the end of a ten-year period.

Whipple started by relating the facts of Wesley's sad childhood in detail, describing his lonely trip back to his father's house after his mother died, and reading aloud testimonials from neighbors about the abuse and neglect Wesley had suffered there. He appealed to his colleagues to imagine themselves in the position of the boy: isolated and without the comfort of friends or family, capable of only the most crude and immature reasoning, and desperate to escape. Common sense, he argued, would suggest that a child, under these circumstances and at such a young age, was not capable of adult reasoning. At the time of the crime, Whipple noted, no one had advocated for Wesley, and his lawyer had ignored the common law rule that presumed children were innocent of crimes. Whipple argued that Wesley should never have been convicted of the crime of murder and sentencing him to life in prison had been illegal and unjust.

Whipple turned from the law to focus on Wesley's transformation in prison. He described reports from the wardens and from Harlan, and then closed his argument by reading aloud one of Wesley's letters, declaring it more erudite than any legislator could compose. According to the newspapers, the letter produced a "profound impression" on the audience, with some moved to tears. Whipple's address was later said to be "one of the most masterly speeches of the session," establishing him as a prominent leader of the Senate in the years to come.

Senator Hiram Bishop responded with the case against Wesley, referring to him as Dr. Jekyll and Mr. Hyde: the split personality with the good side masking the evil within. Wesley presented himself now as Dr. Jekyll, Bishop argued, with his handsome countenance and educated words. But evidence of his true character—as the malicious Mr. Hyde—was demonstrated by his appalling crime. As Bishop described the bloody details, he acted out the role, reaching below the table and bringing forth a wooden club stained with dark spots. He raised the weapon dramatically over his head and swung it through the air in a downward motion. In thunderous tones, Bishop declared that the club was the actual weapon used by Wesley to beat his stepmother to death.

The tension of the moment was broken by a childish voice. Bishop's three-year-old daughter freed herself from her mother's arms in the audience and ran down the center aisle of the chamber, calling out "Mamma, mamma, papa's saying something!" Laughter rippled through the gallery, and according to one newspaper report, senators applauded for the child who displayed "a zest that the father might well envy." Someone near the front of the chamber stopped the child and quickly led her back to her mother.

After only a moment's hesitation, Bishop resumed his address. Again, he challenged the idea that a true degenerate could ever change, repeating the idea that criminality could be inherited. The possibility that he might marry and multiply was to Bishop one of the most serious issues. Any woman who married him would wreck her life, and "God pity the offspring of that marriage."

Bishop called out Professor Harlan by name, claiming that his support of Wesley had proved he was "a sentimentalist dwelling in an atmosphere of exclusiveness that [makes] him unfit for the practical things of the world." In sneering tones, Bishop related a question he had put to Professor Harlan, asking if he would allow his own daughter to marry Wesley Elkins. Harlan had responded: "Senator Bishop, I have no daughter, but I have often said to Mrs. Harlan that if I did have, I should not want any young man to court and marry her." Despite laughter from the audience, Bishop condemned Harlan for ignoring the question, and "casting reflection upon many good men in Iowa."

Bishop's speech was not as well received as he had hoped. Some senators objected to Bishop's display of the weapon, his hyperbolic language, and his reliance on local rumors. Many felt that his attack on Professor Harlan was undeserved. Back in Mount Vernon, the *Cornellian* praised Professor Harlan for his humorous response and denounced Bishop for his words.

Throughout the day, other senators rose to express their views. While several agreed with Bishop, more of them rose to condemn the intolerance and narrow-mindedness that seemed to underlie the opposition. By the end, the arguments supporting Wesley proved to be most convincing. The final tally, taken late that afternoon, was 27 to 20 in favor of the resolution recommending parole. His supporters and nearly all in the gallery left the capital congratulating each other and in high spirits.

The *Des Moines Daily Capital* reported the victory for Wesley under the headline "SENATE VOTES TO RELEASE THE CHILD MURDERER." The next challenge would come on the floor of the House.

20.

THE HOUSE OF REPRESENTATIVES commenced its debate the following day, and as in the Senate, the gallery was crowded with observers. Wesley's supporters were optimistic, reporting that favorable sentiment was even stronger in the House than in the Senate. As in previous days, the speeches were passionate and emotional, captivating the attention of the onlookers. Supporters cited legal precedent on Wesley's side, while also appealing for empathy and compassion.

Dr. Bert Eiker, a thirty-year-old physician from Decatur, urged his colleagues to remember the immaturity of an eleven-year-old child. He displayed photographs of Wesley at that age, and he called on a young page named Bertie Winslow—also age eleven—to distribute the pictures throughout the gallery. Bertie Winslow was a great favorite in the House, described in a newspaper report as "the picture of childish innocence and honest, open frankness." As Winslow came forward, Eiker spoke:

> I want you to remember that this boy here . . . is of exactly the same age, is of about the height and build as was Wesley Elkins at the time the crime was committed. I ask you if this boy were this night to commit a crime so foul as the one committed by Wesley, would you—could you, declare that he was capable of discerning between right and wrong and of clearly reasoning the duty and relations he owes to his fellow man?

BURTON SWEET, representative from Bremer, was another powerful speaker on Wesley's behalf. Representative Sweet, thirty-five years old, was a lawyer in his second term in the House of Representatives. A graduate of Cornell College, Sweet was well acquainted with Professor James Harlan, but he had disagreed with him initially on the pardon question. At Harlan's suggestion, he had studied the case, approaching it with a lawyer-like thoroughness; perusing legal documents and testimony from witnesses; collecting newspaper reports; and researching the law on children and criminal intent. His investigation, along with a visit to Wesley, had persuaded Sweet to change his mind.

In his address to the House, Sweet presented his findings in meticulous detail, explaining how they justified a recommendation in favor of parole. Sweet was convinced that legal precedent was on Wesley's side: he read excerpts from court cases in Iowa and elsewhere, with judges deciding that a child was not of "discriminating legal age," and so could not be found guilty of murder. He urged legislators to ignore the fearmongering and unfounded rumors in Clayton County.

Burton Sweet was a skilled public speaker, practiced in arguing before juries. As a competent litigator, he knew that facts and legal arguments could not always persuade, and he ended his speech with a dramatic appeal:

> It has been said that we know something of ourselves; that we know something of the average man. We know something of his failures, we know something of his successes, his triumphs, something of his defeats. . . . We do not know in what mysterious realm the clouds gather which dim and darken all the heavens of the brain, which, in an unguarded moment, and quick as the lightning's flash, the terrible deed is done that leaves a curse, an everlasting curse, upon the soul. Our ignorance should make us hesitate. Our weakness should make us merciful.

According to the *Daily Capital*, Sweet's speech was ranked with the very best efforts of the day, and the audience applauded when he finished.

When Sweet took his seat, a page tapped him on the shoulder and handed him a note signed by Governor Cummins. Although many legislators believed that Cummins, who was in the audience, would be against the parole, the governor had written: "You can say this if you want to. I will not turn down the legislature if the resolution is passed. I will parole him if the legislature so recommends." Sweet did not divulge the contents of the note to his colleagues. He folded the piece of paper and put it in his pocket.

Another particularly memorable speech came from Colonel Samuel Moore, the representative from Davis County and the oldest legislator at eighty-one years of age. Moore was a decorated Civil War veteran and a popular speaker, known as "the silvertongued orator of the House." He recounted an incident from his own childhood, telling how he had been "beaten and abused" by boys who were physically stronger than him. According to the newspaper report, people in the audience wiped away tears as they listened to Colonel Moore describe his overwhelming anger and how he had been "driven to desperation" and come close to violence. Even now he remembered the difficulty of maintaining self-control, and he asserted that the provocations in Wesley's childhood were so much more severe.

Not all were persuaded by the emotional speeches such as Moore's. One reporter overheard a legislator's sarcastic remark: "If we are to pardon every prisoner who asks for his release, let us act on them en masse: Let us free the entire population of our penitentiaries, turn them into institutions of the feeble minded and send the legislature to occupy them."

Opposition to Wesley was led principally by J. C. Flenniken, one of the few Republicans elected from Clayton County. Flenniken was thirty-nine years old, in his first term in the General Assembly, and he had worked hard to make friends. By the time the debate started, he had obtained pledges from some of his colleagues to join with him to vote against parole. Flenniken was optimistic that the final vote would go his way.

Flenniken was a jewelry tradesman with little experience as a public speaker. As expected, he emphasized the passionate feelings in his county, brandishing a thick stack of petitions signed by 1,700 Clayton County citizens against Wesley's parole. Flenniken claimed to have spoken to Judge Hoyt who had sentenced Wesley to life in prison, and the judge agreed that Wesley should remain where he was. Furthermore, Flenniken declared, Wesley was still under indictment for the murder of his stepmother, and he would be arrested on that charge if he returned to Clayton County.

When his time had nearly expired, Flenniken produced a copy of the damning article from the *Des Moines Daily Leader* emphasizing Wesley's background. He proceeded to slowly read it aloud, continuing even as the audience and his fellow legislators grew restless. Finally, the Speaker of the House rapped his gavel. After consulting with other representatives, the Speaker allowed Flenniken to carry on. Others on his side were forced to shorten their remarks, adding little to arguments that had been made before.

Eventually, the vote was called, and the names were read. Observers kept track of the vote, many quietly voicing their approval when the numbers went in Wesley's direction. As the tally neared the end, the room grew silent, and when the Speaker announced the final result, some in the gallery gasped while others sat in disbelief. The resolution for parole was defeated by a single vote, with the count standing at 47 to 46. The reporter from the *Daily Capital* rushed out to write a story for the paper that was quickly published with the headline "WESLEY ELKINS TOLD TO PIN HIS FAITH ON FUTURE ASSEMBLIES."

The fight, however, was not over. After a brief pause, Polk County's Representative Horace Teachout, one of the "nay" votes, rose from his seat and motioned to Representative Sweet. The two men spoke quietly for a few moments, and Teachout explained that he was ready to change his vote. He had pledged his initial vote to Flenniken, and he had now fulfilled his promise. In a dramatic and unexpected move, Sweet took the floor and moved that the resolution should be reconsidered and a second vote taken. The audience listened in rapt attention as people waited to see if the motion would pass. Apparently, Teachout was not the only person having second thoughts, and the motion was approved. The next day, House members would cast ballots a second time on the resolution to grant Wesley his parole.

Wesley's supporters spent the evening visiting colleagues, urging them to follow Teachout's lead, and in the morning, some legislators were conspicuously absent from their desks. Even Flenniken from Clayton County recognized that the tide had turned. In the end, the number in favor of Wesley increased by only two, but the total opposed fell sharply, with ten representatives choosing to abstain.

With the final vote at 48 to 35, the Speaker proclaimed that the resolution had passed; the House majority concurred with the decision by the Senate. The General Assembly would now recommend to Governor Cummins that John Wesley Elkins be paroled.

21.

GOVERNOR CUMMINS was notified shortly after the House vote. Within minutes a telegram was composed and transmitted to Warden Hunter.

A group of men who backed the conditional parole approached the governor and requested that Wesley be released immediately so he could travel to Des Moines and personally thank the legislators who supported him. Cummins turned down the request. The *Republican*, a newspaper that had advocated on behalf of Wesley, supported the governor's decision in a column titled "NO HEROIZING." The paper took the position that "It is to the credit of Governor Cummins that he turned down such a proposal. The governor informed the boy worshippers that he should be paroled just the same as any other convict is paroled."

Now finally, after his fourth appeal, upon learning that he would be released, Wesley sat down to do what he did best. He wrote a letter and asked that it be sent to Senator Whipple, one of Wesley's most visible and consistent supporters. Similar to Wesley's other letters, this one was eloquent, formal, and humble.

On April 7, Senator Whipple walked from his office to the floor of the Senate in the gold-domed capitol building. He requested that Wesley's letter be read aloud on the Senate floor. When permission was granted, he gave the letter to a page, who carried it to the front of the chamber and handed it to Secretary Newman.

Newman glanced over the letter and began to read in a strong and steady voice:

My Dear Sir:

I desire to extend my earnest and heartfelt thanks to you and
to say a few words in acknowledgement of the thoughtful and
careful examination into the merits of my parole appeal. I shall
ever be a debtor to you for your painstaking care in getting at
the facts of the case. . . .

Newman paused, his voice breaking. The chamber was still,
except for the shuffling of chairs. Newman cleared his throat. He
continued to read.

It will be the sovereign desire and the earnest effort of my life
to justify the judgment and faithful efforts of my friends. . . .
To those who at present are opposed I appeal to them to withhold their judgment until I have time to demonstrate outside
of these walls whether my pretensions of leading a life upright
in character, strong and thoughtful, gentlemanly always, are
genuine or false, and I can confidently believe at the end of ten
years they will hasten to commend the action of the Twenty-
Ninth General Assembly of Iowa.

Very respectfully and gratefully, Wesley Elkins

The emotion of the moment gripped the men in the room. Wesley's words deeply affected many of the legislators. Newspaper
reporters who were in the room told their readers that several
senators were brought to tears.

In most of the state, especially in Des Moines and places where
Professor Harlan was well known, the public was pleased by the
decision and congratulated the General Assembly for its action.
Some newspapers condemned the opposition's exaggerated fears,
and a few commentators proclaimed that Wesley's imprisonment
had been illegal from the beginning.

The citizens of Clayton County, however, responded angrily to
what they saw as the denigration of their fears. Residents wanted

Wesley to remember that he had been sentenced only for the murder of his father. The *Elkader Argus* warned:

> It is not a secret that the Clayton County authorities may arrest Wesley if they get hold of him. . . . The indictment [for the murder of his stepmother] still hangs over him, and there is little or no disposition on the part of his old neighbors to forget it or forego it. If they could bring Wesley back, he would be brought . . . to this county in short order and put on trial again."

TWO FULL WEEKS elapsed before the official papers arrived at Anamosa with the conditions of the parole. Although Wesley's release was imminent, he was still required to follow the daily routines of the institution. He was awakened each day at 6:30, walked silently to the dining hall for breakfast and then to his work assignment. He ate a wordless dinner and returned to his cell to sleep.

One evening he was escorted by a guard to the prison tailor where he was fitted for a suit of civilian clothes. Just as he had done twelve years earlier, he stood in front of the tailor and was measured from head to toe. He was now five feet, three-and-a-half inches tall—having grown almost nine inches during his confinement—and he was slender, weighing about 120 pounds.

Wesley stood with his arms outstretched so the tailor could measure his sleeve length. Holding his pencil in his mouth, the tailor assessed Wesley's inseam, neck size, and the circumference of his head, and recorded the numbers on a scrap of paper. When the tailor was finished, the guard took Wesley back to his cell.

On April 14, 1902, Governor Cummins signed the order to release Wesley Elkins. The document, titled "THE GOVERNOR'S ORDER OF SUSPENSION OF SENTENCE," was sent by B. W. Garrett, the Pardon Secretary, to Professor Harlan. A message was also delivered to Warden Hunter, telling him that Harlan would arrive at

Anamosa Penitentiary on Saturday, April 19, to present the order
and take Wesley away.

The legislature had recommended a conditional parole, and
Wesley had promised many times to comply with all conditions
imposed, no matter how drastic. As official parole papers typically
required, the parolee was to avoid intoxicating liquors, obey the
laws, and write to the governor at least once a month. Furthermore, Wesley was not allowed to charge money for public appearances, and he was to reside in Linn County, home of Professor
Harlan, unless granted permission by the governor. Wesley's
parole papers included one unique provision, forbidding him to
enter the county where the crime occurred or adjacent counties.
That would not be a burden to Wesley, who knew he could be in
danger if he were to revisit Clayton County. Wesley focused on one
of the final sentences in the document, promising that if he complied with the requirements for ten years, he would be granted a
full and unconditional pardon.

Harlan hoped that the transfer could be accomplished with a
minimum of public knowledge or scrutiny. He was sensitive to the
fact that Wesley's release would be viewed unfavorably by some,
and he wanted to spare Wesley any confrontation with his antag-
onists. So instead of driving his carriage on Saturday morning to
Anamosa—a distance of seventeen miles from Mount Vernon—
Harlan chose to go to the prison on Friday evening.

A gentle rain fell that afternoon as the horses plodded along
the muddy roads underneath an overcast sky, giving way to a
gradual clearing. Harlan reached the prison around 6 P.M. and
went immediately to Warden Hunter's residence to deliver the
official papers. Hunter reviewed the documents and excused himself, walking across the prison yard to Wesley's cell to tell him the
news. The warden later reported that when he walked outside he
saw a perfect rainbow appearing in an arc over the prison walls.

That evening Harlan and Hunter dined together and discussed
the logistics of Wesley's discharge in the morning. At 7:30 P.M., a

young man named Frank Moorhead appeared at the front door and announced that he was a reporter from the *Des Moines Daily Capital*. He had been dispatched by the newspaper to cover the story of Wesley's release the next morning. As Professor Harlan later wrote to the governor, "I was very sorry that I did not get into Anamosa and out without being seen by a reporter, but the fates were against me."

SOON AFTER Hunter had conveyed the news of Harlan's arrival, a guard unlocked Wesley's cell door and accompanied him to the prison barbershop. Wesley climbed into the chair, and the barber, a fellow prisoner, covered him with a cloth. The barber cut Wesley's hair, and lathered and shaved his face, washing it with a warm towel. For the last time, Wesley ate his evening meal in the company of his fellow prisoners. Then, as he had done for more than 4,500 nights, Wesley lay down on the straw mattress in his cell and slept.

Whenever a prisoner was pardoned or paroled, the news was publicized in the *Prison Press* and welcomed by other convicts, giving them hope for their future. Wesley Elkins, who had been at Anamosa for twelve years, was well known to them as their librarian, and he was respected for his work ethic, his studious nature, and his good behavior. Prisoners and guards cheered when they heard that John Wesley Elkins, the prison's most prominent member, was about to be released from the penitentiary.

SATURDAY MORNING dawned clear and bright, a cloudless blue sky. Wesley ate breakfast then returned to his cell. As he was instructed, he took off his prison uniform and dressed in new clothes: a white shirt, a blue bat-wing tie, and the blue serge suit made by the prison tailor. Sitting on the edge of his bed, Wesley laced up a new pair of shoes. Leaving his cell for the last time, he carried an overcoat and a small satchel, and he wore a new fawn Fedora hat. Wesley was used to prison caps, and he frequently reached up, pulling the unfamiliar hat from side to side and backward and forward, trying to adjust it to his head.

Before leaving the prison, Deputy Warden Gurley took Wesley to the prison library where Wesley had spent so many hours reading, studying, and composing letters to plead for his freedom. Now twenty-three years old, Wesley sat on a simple wooden chair in front of bookcases and posed for the photographer. In the photo, sunlight streams into the room, and Wesley is angled toward the camera. His left leg is crossed over his right leg, and his right arm is bent and propped casually on the back of the chair. He holds a scroll or document of some kind—perhaps the parole papers—in his left hand. His hair is neatly parted and carefully combed, and he looks directly at the camera without definite expression.

After the photograph, Deputy Warden Gurley led Wesley to the discharge clerk, who gave him five dollars, the standard amount the state provided for convicts being set free. A turnkey unlocked the inner and outer gates to allow Wesley and the deputy warden to pass into the public area of the prison administration building. They walked across the marble floor to Warden Hunter's office, where they were greeted by a group of five men: Warden Hunter; the warden's brother; the warden's private secretary, Mr. Churchill; Professor Harlan; and Mr. Moorhead, the reporter from the *Daily Capital*. Each of them shook hands with Wesley.

Wesley stood in front of Warden Hunter with his eyes directed at the floor as the warden read aloud the paper signed by Governor Cummins.

"Wesley, do you agree to be bound by the terms of this parole?" Hunter asked.

Wesley could not look up or speak. He coughed, cleared his throat, and nodded in agreement.

Warden Hunter spoke again: "I have refrained from congratulating you before. But I want to do it now. You're a free man now." He stepped forward, and once again, shook hands with Wesley.

"Thank you," Wesley said softly.

Wesley Elkins, seated in the library of the Anamosa State Penitentiary, where he spent many hours reading, writing, studying, and overseeing the circulation of materials. It is likely the photo was taken on the day of his release in April 1902. (Courtesy of Steve Wendl and the Anamosa State Penitentiary Prison History website.)

Hunter guided Wesley outside onto the prison's portico where Mrs. Hunter was waiting. She wished Wesley good luck and a safe journey.

In the street, a convict labor crew was repairing the street. A guard, armed with a double-barreled Winchester, kept a steady watch over the prisoners.

Harlan and Wesley descended the steps. Wesley carried the satchel with his personal belongings, and he clutched a package under his arm.

Moorhead was waiting for them, and Harlan agreed to a brief stop. When the reporter asked about the package, Wesley told him that he was carrying two books that Professor Harlan had given him; they had been his great companions in prison. He volunteered that he had read books of all kinds: fiction, biography, travel, and adventure. When he was asked about his future, Wesley said that he would do whatever the professor suggested; he would always follow his advice. Wesley went on to say that his greatest wish was "to succeed so I can prove to the people that I am deserving of this trust they have placed in me, and that I can live down my past life."

Then Professor Harlan guided Wesley to the waiting buggy.

Warden Hunter accompanied them. In parting, he told Professor Harlan: "Be sure you treat Wesley right. We won't have him mistreated, you know. He's too good a boy for that."

Hunter also offered Wesley some final words of advice. "Don't look back, Wesley," he said. "Never look back, always go ahead."

Someone else called out, "I'm sorry, Wesley, we haven't any rice to throw after you. That will come later in your life."

"He probably doesn't know what that means," said Deputy Warden Gurley.

Harlan and Wesley climbed into the buggy. Harlan shook the reins, and the horses started to move.

The guard with the convict labor crew raised his shotgun to present arms and saluted as the buggy passed by. He had the last words for Wesley: "Goodbye, Wesley. Be a good boy."

REDEMPTION
1902–1961

22.

THE TRIP FROM Anamosa to Mount Vernon took approximately four hours. The countryside between the two towns was mostly flat with farmhouses and outbuildings set well back from the road. Wesley could see farmers working in the wet earth, completing the task of spring planting.

Professor Harlan and Wesley arrived in Mount Vernon in the early afternoon. The horses pulling Harlan's buggy clomped up a steep incline leading to the center of town. Harlan steered the horses to the right onto Main Street. Ninety feet wide with rows of brick buildings on both sides, the rough dirt road was muddy from the previous day's rain. Although the street wasn't famous yet, it would be incorporated into the Lincoln Highway in 1913, the first national memorial to honor the country's sixteenth president: a coast-to-coast gravel road from Times Square in New York to Lincoln Park in San Francisco.

In a letter to Governor Cummins, Harlan noted that Wesley enjoyed the ride. That would have been an understatement; Wesley must have been exhilarated as well as a bit frightened. After twelve years of confinement, he had been released from the stone-walled prison that had been his home when he was a child and throughout his entire adolescence. Now, as a young adult, he was riding through a thriving American small town. Residents walked the streets, and perhaps a few raised their hands in greeting as they recognized Harlan and his carriage passing by. Wesley was far removed from iron cell doors that slammed shut at night, armed guards, and restrictions on what he could say, who he could speak to, and where he could walk.

Harlan guided the buggy through the downtown, passing Platner's hardware store and tin shop, the law office of Charles Kepler, the Mount Vernon Bank, a clothing store, bakery, shoe store, meat market, other businesses, and several churches. A half mile to the west, the grounds of Cornell College could be seen: wide and welcoming lawns shaded by sturdy oaks; Old Sem, a rectangular brick building with a mansard roof that was the first structure on campus; and the magnificent chapel, featuring a 130-foot main tower with a Seth Thomas clock. The gray stone exterior of the chapel was built of the same dolomitic limestone used to construct the walls of Anamosa State Penitentiary.

The Harlans lived on the southwest edge of campus in a neat and square two-and-half-story wood frame house with scalloped trim on the peaks. Professor Harlan pulled his buggy to a stop at the back of the house. His wife, Janette, emerged from the kitchen door and greeted Wesley in the yard. Harlan observed that Wesley seemed nervous when they showed him around the house and grounds.

For the first time in twelve years, Wesley would sleep outside prison walls. He had a room of his own, without the scrutiny of guards. Wesley had a new home.

ON APRIL 19, 1902, the day Wesley left Anamosa, a long article written by Frank Moorhead, the reporter who was on the scene for Wesley's departure from Anamosa, was published in the *Des Moines Daily Capital*. Following the bitter legislative debate, the article attracted attention throughout the state. When it was reprinted in the *Mount Vernon Hawkeye,* it introduced residents to the young man who would now be living in their midst.

Most people in Mount Vernon knew little about Wesley other than what they had read in the newspapers. The details of his violent crime had been repeated many times, so they understood that he had been convicted of killing his parents, and some people believed he was dangerous. The article portrayed Wesley in a different light, depicting him as a deferential and shy young man who longed for support and encouragement. The reporter noted Warden Hunter's account of Wesley as a model prisoner, as well as Professor Harlan's confidence that Wesley would prove himself worthy of freedom.

Moorhead included a description of the young man:

> Elkins was wrapped up in a great ulster which completely enveloped him. . . . He is about 5 feet 2 inches tall, weighs only about 110 pounds and looks decidedly frail. He is a good looking man, clear faced and dark haired, with only one thing against his looks, that being his eyes, which are too deep set and too close together. But as to any look of the degeneracy which his enemies hold against him, there is none.

Moorhead imagined the challenges Wesley would face:

> He must learn to think and to plan his own time and not be dependent upon time locks and clanking chains for his hourly actions. He knows no more of the customs of other people who are free than a little child. . . . He must learn to walk down the streets of Mt. Vernon with the lockstep only as a memory; he must learn to walk abreast of Prof. Harlan and his other associates and not immediately behind him with chest touching back, legs and knees crooked together and right hand resting on the shoulder of his guardian in front. He must learn when he walks desultorily not to take the customary six paces front, then reverse and to the rear, showing the confines of his prison cell and the former limitations of his freedom. Elkins must even learn to talk.

One week after they arrived in Mount Vernon, Professor Harlan wrote a letter to Governor Cummins, updating him about Wesley's status. He informed him that Wesley was doing well and seemed ready and anxious to begin his studies. In order to encourage independence, Harlan had told him that he would have to earn his board by working around the house and garden, and by doing odd jobs for others in the community. One professor from Cornell College had already offered the young man a small task, and Wesley was proud to show Mrs. Harlan the sum of thirty cents he had received.

After this brief report to the governor, Harlan raised a question. Did the governor think it advisable for Wesley to move?

The parole papers stated that Wesley would stay in Mount Vernon unless the governor permitted him to leave, and Harlan and Cummins had agreed that he would live with the Harlans, at least temporarily. Wesley could start school there, and Harlan could keep a close eye on him. Also, they hoped Wesley would meet young people close to his age who could see past his history and accept him as a fellow student.

Both Harlan and the governor, however, were aware of the hostility toward Wesley in Clayton County, and they feared that rumors circulating there might take root in Mount Vernon. Harlan remembered the governor had commented that Wesley might do better if he lived in a different state, and an opportunity had now presented itself.

Professor Harlan wrote that he had heard from a former Cornell College professor who was now living in New York City. This man was interested in Wesley's case and offered to look after Wesley if he could move and continue his studies there.

Harlan didn't give his own opinion of the idea, and we couldn't locate the governor's response or anything that identified this person. We don't know whether the two men gave serious consideration to the idea, or whether Wesley was ever told of the letter.

THROUGHOUT THE spring and summer of 1902, Wesley adjusted to a new routine and way of life. After a few restless nights, he slept soundly. He ate his meals with Professor and Mrs. Harlan, and he took on small tasks for them and for their neighbors. Wesley looked forward to the end of August, when he would begin his formal education.

Cornell College had been founded in 1853, and its progressive reputation was well-established. In 1858, the college's first graduating class consisted of one woman and one man, who later married each other. Eighteen years after its founding, the college was the first in the country to have a female full professor earning the same salary as men on the faculty. In the 1870s, Cornell admitted Black students, and the trustees officially declared that race would not be a factor in admissions. In later years, Frederick Douglass, Elizabeth Cady Stanton, Susan B. Anthony, and Booker T. Washington gave lectures on campus. Cornell encouraged diversity and set high intellectual standards. Given the open-mindedness of students and administrators, Professor Harlan, who was Vice President of the college in 1902, believed that Cornell was a place where Wesley could thrive.

When Wesley arrived on campus in 1902, men and women congregated in separate groups. Contact between the sexes was limited. Until 1895, they were not permitted to walk together on campus or in town without first getting special permission. Rules dictated student behavior, including a strange prohibition against urinating in the snow. Other restrictions forbade dancing, gambling, playing cards, leaving campus without permission, and failing to observe study hours. Smoking was discouraged but tolerated. Wesley, who was used to following the rules of an institution, had no trouble adjusting.

Cornell's campus was dominated by the impressive chapel, completed in time for dedication and graduation ceremonies in June 1882. The main room was large enough to seat nearly 1,000 people, and the space was often filled with the sounds coming from the 3,800 pipes of a Moller organ.

College Hall, the main classroom building on campus, stood on the eastern edge of the college grounds. Unfortunately, Cornell did not have a free-standing library in 1902. After spending so many hours in the quiet and well-stocked prison library—its inventory had increased to nearly 7,000 books—Wesley missed such a place at Cornell. There were, however, much smaller libraries maintained in the rooms occupied by the four literary societies: two for men, two for women.

Wesley joined one of these groups soon after he started school, and he spent many hours immersed in books. He realized how much had changed while he was at Anamosa. As a young man with a deep curiosity and an intellectual bent, he took advantage of this opportunity to educate himself on contemporary events.

FOR AMERICANS, the world had changed markedly in the last decade of the nineteenth century. Banks and businesses failed, setting off the Panic of 1893 and causing widespread economic depression and a national crisis. Railroads went bankrupt. Homeowners who could no longer afford their mortgages walked away from the houses they once owned. In 1894, Coxey's Army of unemployed workers marched on Washington, D.C.

Jim Crow laws and laws restricting the voting rights of Blacks were enacted in many southern states. Racial segregation was legally enforced, and in 1896, the Supreme Court decided *Plessy v. Ferguson*, upholding the constitutionality of those laws.

At the end of the decade, international tensions flared, and wars broke out overseas in Europe and the Far East. The sinking of the USS *Maine* in Havana harbor in 1898 led to the Spanish-American War.

There were also positive developments. Inventors experimented with flying machines and engines attached to gliders as humans began to explore the possibility of air travel. In Massachusetts, the Duryea brothers developed the first gasoline-powered car and began the commercial production of automobiles. Thomas Edison's invention of the kinetoscope would eventually contribute to the motion picture industry.

In September 1901, seven months before Wesley was released from prison, President William McKinley was shot and mortally wounded at the Temple of Music on the grounds of the Pan-

American Exposition in Buffalo, New York. Theodore Roosevelt succeeded McKinley. As president, Roosevelt argued for progressive reforms, especially regarding business and the regulation of economic activity. Railroads were the dominant industry of the era, with the capacity to move people and goods faster and more efficiently than any other means. Roosevelt's concern about the economic power of the industry and the ethics of these business owners dominated the early years of his presidency.

The Progressive Era, lasting through the 1920s, saw the rise of various social reform movements that began to transform and shape the ways Americans viewed themselves and their obligations to others. Suffragettes continued to demonstrate for the rights of women to vote and hold office. Social scientists and others argued that children should be treated differently under the law, and reformers urged state legislatures to authorize separate juvenile courts and reformatories.

UNDER THE terms of his parole, Wesley was required to write monthly letters to the governor of Iowa during the ten years after his release, reporting on his activities, plans, and aspirations. His first letter was dated May 1902, his last April 1912. All were carefully filed and preserved by the pardon secretary in the office of the governor and eventually transferred to the archives of the State Historical Society of Iowa. "Answered" is the notation on the top of each one. Unfortunately, none of the responses to Wesley's letters can be found in the archives.

What we know about Wesley Elkins during the ten years from 1902 until 1912—after he left Anamosa as a young man of twenty-three and matured into an adult in his early thirties—comes from this trove of letters.

Wesley had demonstrated his fine persuasive writing skills in the long and expressive letters he wrote from Anamosa, designed to persuade and appeal to readers' emotions. In contrast, the ones he wrote to the governor tended to be short and recited facts.

Most were handwritten; a few were typed. Always deferential, he typically signed his letters "Most Respectfully Yours." He was careful with grammar, and he was nearly always timely, dating his letters on the 19th of each month, the anniversary of his departure from Anamosa. The few times he was one or two days late, he apologized for the delay.

Occasionally Wesley expressed anxieties—most often about money, his health, and his future—and he asked for advice. He often wrote of how grateful he was for the opportunities he had been given. A diligent worker, Wesley was always modest, noting achievements briefly and without conceit.

Although he left Anamosa in 1902, Wesley's struggle for redemption continued long after his release. He knew that some people believed he was a threat to society and should have remained behind bars. For the next ten years—until he was eligible for an unconditional pardon—he would seek to prove that he deserved his freedom.

23.

WESLEY'S FIRST LETTER, addressed to the Hon. A. B. Cummins, was written in May 1902. Although only a month had passed since he left Anamosa, Wesley was already focused on how to provide for himself. Encouraged by Professor Harlan, Mount Vernon residents hired Wesley to work in their homes and on their grounds. Wesley kept careful records of his income, earning $9.45 in June and $13.15 in July. In his fourth letter to Governor Cummins, dated August 19, 1902, Wesley was proud to report that a Cornell professor and his wife had asked him to housesit for ten weeks, spending nights there while the couple was out of town.

Wesley also noted that he was taking the opportunity to meet people. He was attending the Methodist church regularly, had gone to several meetings of young members of the congregation, and was investigating the college literary societies. Although the semester was still several weeks away, he wanted the governor to know that he was serious about his education. As he wrote, "I have not taken up any formal line of study yet but expect to do so in a few days."

At the end of the summer, Professor Harlan decided that Wesley should enroll in Cornell Academy, later renamed Cornell College High School. Because of the few educational opportunities in the state, the Academy had been founded in 1853, at the same time as the college. The Academy accepted students who had graduated from the lower grades and offered courses in liberal arts designed to prepare them for college-level work. It also included a business curriculum to train students to enter the job force. Cornell College and Cornell Academy shared the same buildings, and often the same professors taught classes at both levels. High school and college students mingled and socialized together.

Students entering the Academy varied widely in their levels of education, and pre-college academic programs were typically shaped to meet individual needs. They might need anywhere from one to four years to complete the program. Wesley was eager to graduate from the preparatory school and start college, but he also wanted to support himself. Business courses, he thought, would be most useful in finding a steady job, and he registered for a full load, including stenography, typewriting, bookkeeping, and grammar. He planned to take classes in commercial law and banking later in the year. According to his calculations, it would take him seven years to graduate with a college degree and would cost nearly $1,200 in tuition. In order to earn money, Wesley took part-time jobs preparing bulletins and inserts for the local newspaper, working at a dry-cleaning store, and helping in the office of the college registrar.

In mid-October 1902, only a month after enrolling in school, Wesley was voted in as a member of the Gladstone Literary Society. The literary societies were the most important student groups at Cornell. They were responsible for the student newspaper and for selecting the editors. Collegiate debate and oratory contests were popular in Iowa at the time, and the societies took the lead in preparing contestants. The Cornell teams were known to be fierce competitors, and members spent long hours studying politics and international affairs and engaging in lengthy conversations with their peers. The societies held business meetings, enforced strict parliamentary rules, and sponsored public programs to encourage spirited exchanges of ideas and practice in public speaking.

Many students spent more time involved in their societies than on their course work, and members of the Gladstone Society were no exception. Faculty members were increasingly concerned about the imbalance, and in 1904, administrators would enact a rule limiting society members from participating in more than one debate a year.

Since fraternities were not allowed at Cornell, the literary societies also played an important role in the social life of the college. According to a college yearbook, the friendships among the members lasted long past graduation: "In defeat or victory, the feeling of society brotherhood only deepens, and the spirit of loyalty never wavers."

The bonds were strengthened by the separate cheers developed over the years by each society. When Wesley joined, he was required to learn the one identifying his group. The Gladstone page in the Cornell yearbook featured Gladstone's "yell":

Re-Rah-Rell!
Hear Us Yell!
We're the Gladstones!
Caw-Caw-Nell!

While Wesley was at Anamosa, he had had no opportunity to speak in public. Nevertheless, he undertook the challenge of preparing for debates during his first year at Cornell. Despite only two months of practice, he won one of his first debate contests in November 1902, and he was soon challenged to another on women's suffrage.

During the spring semester of 1903, Wesley achieved two great successes. In March, members of the Gladstone Society elected him as their secretary. Two months later, they chose him as one of three men to compete in the debate against the Irving Society scheduled for the following December. It was a significant accomplishment. The debate would be widely publicized, and the college printed special stationery with the letterhead "Cornell College Ninth Annual Inter-Society Debate, Gladstone-Irving." Wesley's name was listed with the other two members on his team, and Wesley used this stationery for his next eight letters to Governor Cummins.

In May 1903, Cornell marked the end of the academic year with social events. Wesley attended five concerts at the three-day music festival and volunteered to serve as an usher. In June 1903, he wrote to the governor, "I certainly am very keenly appreciative of the privileges I have enjoyed in the past year and I trust I am stronger and better able to fight the battles of life more than when I entered Cornell."

Although he had been in school for less than a year, Wesley had grown comfortable at Cornell. He had kept busy with his school-work and activities involving other students, and he was lonely when they left for the summer. The close of school, he told the governor in June, "brings a level of sadness I had not anticipated and I should be glad when it again opens in September."

Soon after Wesley wrote that letter, he was invited by Cora Bassett, his half-sister, to spend a month with her in Blooming Prairie, Minnesota. Although Cora had offered to take Wesley in upon his release from prison, she knew that legislators had de-cided that he should stay in Linn County under the guidance of Professor Harlan. But she hoped that Wesley could visit her and meet her family. Wesley would also be able to see Mark, his half-brother, who was living and working on a farm nearby.

Cora and Mark were John Elkins' children by his first wife, Phoebe, and the three siblings had not been together for many years. Wesley was seven years old and living with his father when Cora left Iowa. He was age eleven when he had last seen Mark.

In the spring of 1903, Wesley was twenty-four years old. Mark was thirty-five and Cora was thirty-three, and they were both mar-ried. Wesley may have seen George Bassett briefly at Cora's wed-ding, but he had not yet met Lottie, who had married Mark after Wesley had been sent to prison. Both Cora and Mark had chil-dren: Cora had three sons, ages seventeen, fifteen and twelve— the middle child was named Wesley after her brother—and Mark had a nine-year-old son named Elmer.

Under the terms of the parole, Wesley was forbidden to leave the state unless the governor agreed, and he sent a second letter to Governor Cummins in June to ask permission to visit his sister and brother. He wrote:

Blooming Prairie is not far from the state line, and we would
all like very much to get together once more. . . . My sister
has been in Minn. for a good many years but my brother has
recently moved there on a farm. I think if I could help him with
his work this summer, it would help to make me stronger and
better able to take up school work in the fall as I am greatly in
need of outdoor work.

It would be hard for you to realize how miserable and home-
sick I get at times boarding and rooming out all the time. To get
into a home and realize that it is my home would be a pleasure
I have not experienced for many a long year and if you will
arrange for me to spend the vacation with my brother and sister,
I will feel exceedingly grateful."

Soon after he received the letter from Wesley, Governor Cummins wrote back with his consent.

IN JULY, Wesley took the train from Iowa to Minnesota, arriving
in Blooming Prairie, a small town surrounded by wheat fields,
located on the southeast border of Minnesota. Blooming Prairie
was much like the town of Mount Vernon, with a main street,
depot, general store, blacksmith, several small shops, post office,
and hotel. Residents were still recovering from the Fourth of July
celebration. The population more than quadrupled for the annual
event that featured parades, baseball games, tug-of-war competi-
tions, family picnics, horse races, gambling, and occasional gun-
fire. But the streets were quiet when Wesley arrived.

For nearly nine weeks, Wesley woke early and did hard physical
work under the hot sun. The land was flat and fertile. He may have
been reminded of his boyhood summers outside in rural Iowa,
enduring thick humidity and swarms of mosquitoes during the
days. It stayed light until almost 10 P.M., and the night air was
heavy and dense with fireflies. The black dome of the sky was lit
with distant clusters of stars.

Wesley reported to the governor that the outdoor work was sure to make him "better fitted, physically, to enter vigorously into the duties of the school." Before leaving his sister's home, he wrote: "Minnesota sunshine and air seems to agree with me all right for I am feeling fine and have gained four pounds since leaving Mt. Vernon."

Wesley didn't offer any details about his conversations with Cora and Mark. If anyone knew what had driven Wesley to his crime, it would have been his siblings. They had also lived in their father's house when they were young, both moving away when they were old enough: Cora, when she married, and Mark, when he rented a room and was hired to work on a neighbor's farm. Although Cora and Mark hadn't lived with Wesley in the months before the crime, they would have understood what he had endured as a child.

24.

WESLEY RETURNED TO Iowa in mid-September 1903. On his trip back to Mount Vernon, he stopped in Cedar Falls to meet Nathan Gist, the young boy who had written encouraging and sympathetic letters to him while he was incarcerated at Anamosa. Wesley wanted to express his gratitude in person.

Nathan was now eighteen years old. During the visit, Nathan's father and his wife talked to Wesley and noted his shyness and reserved nature. After thanking Nathan for his kindness, Wesley told him about his summer in Minnesota and his classes at Cornell. He was proud to say that he would be representing one of Cornell's literary societies in a debate contest later that year.

When he returned to Mount Vernon, Wesley chose to register for classes outside of the business curriculum: English, Ancient History, U.S. History, and Political Economy. He worked steadily to prepare for the Gladstone-Irving debate in early December. The question involved tariffs: was the continuance of a protective policy preferable to a policy of a gradual reduction of the tariffs to a revenue basis? The Gladstone Society sponsored trips to help its team prepare, and the three men traveled together to hear from prominent leaders on the subject. They went to Mechanicsville for a presentation by Governor Van Sant of Minnesota, then to Iowa City for a speech by Secretary Shaw, the former Iowa governor now serving as Secretary of the Treasury for President Theodore Roosevelt. In the fall, the team visited Cedar Rapids to hear talks by Robert Cousins, a congressman from Iowa, and by Governor Cummins, who had just been re-elected. The introduction to Cummins—the man who had granted Wesley his parole—must

A photo of the Gladstone Literary Society (1902–1903), published in
The Royal Purple yearbook of Cornell College in 1904. Wesley Elkins
is second from the left, in the second row. (Courtesy of Cole Library/
Cornell College Archives.)

have been a significant moment for Wesley, and he wrote: "I am
very glad that I had the privilege of meeting you as well as the
pleasure of listening to your address. I most cordially congratulate
you upon your re-election to the office of governor."

THAT FALL, the Gladstone Society posed for a group photograph
for the college yearbook. Forty-two men—forty-one white and
one Black—are posed in five rows. All of them are wearing high-
collared white shirts, thin black ties, and jackets buttoned up to
the top. Many of the students have slicked back hair, parted in
the middle. Most are looking straight ahead into the camera, and
none are smiling. Wesley, seated in the second row on the far left,
also has a serious expression. He is one of the few men whose
head is turned slightly, with his eyes focused to the side.

Another yearbook page was devoted to the six members—three
on each team—who competed in the Gladstone-Irving debate. It
featured separate headshots of each man, again dressed in formal
wear. As in the group photograph, Wesley is looking to the side
rather than straight at the camera.

A photo of Wesley Elkins with other debaters who participated in the
Gladstone/Irving debate in December 1903, published in *The Royal Purple*
yearbook of Cornell College in 1905. Wesley Elkins is in the middle of the
bottom row. (Courtesy of Cole Library/Cornell College Archives.)

THE GLADSTONE-IRVING debate was held in December 1903, and
a glowing report was featured prominently in the student newspaper. Wesley was on the Gladstone team arguing for a protective policy, and, when it was his turn, he cited facts showing that
the watch industry, factories, and tin plate plants had prospered
under protection. A reporter noted that "Mr. Elkins' hesitation at
times detracted to a certain extent from the effectiveness of his
argument," and at the end, the judges voted 2 to 1 to award the
victory to the Irving team. The student newspaper commended
both sides, describing the debate as one of the "strongest that had
ever taken place between these two societies."

At the end of the fall semester, Wesley was trusted with increasing responsibilities. Members of the Gladstone Society elected him to be vice president of the group, and chairman of the committee to decide the question to be submitted to the Irving Society for the next debate. Wesley also agreed to serve on the Gladstone-Irving joint committee to draw up a debating constitution, although, as he told the governor, "the society work is a little heavier than I wish to have it."

BY THE END OF 1903—eighteen months after his release from Anamosa Penitentiary—Wesley Elkins was an ambitious and intellectually curious young man. At the age of twenty-five, he was still in his pre-college years and much older than his classmates, but he associated with college students and was a leader in one of the most prestigious groups on campus.

His classmates knew his background. Through the years, he had struggled to have his case brought before the legislature, and the details of the crime had been repeated in newspapers across the state. Did his fellow students whisper about him behind his back? Was he ever challenged to his face about the murders in Clayton County that had shocked the populace of that rural area? Or were the other students able to ignore his past and trust him as one of them, accepting him because of his demeanor, his intellect, and his upstanding behavior?

Nothing in the Cornell archives, in Wesley's letters, or in the papers of Professor Harlan, suggests that Wesley was treated any differently than other students on campus.

25.

WESLEY WAS BEGINNING his second year at Cornell Academy in October 1903 when a short story by the Iowa native Susan Glaspell appeared in *Harper's Magazine*. Initially entitled "In the Face of His Constituents," Glaspell later changed the title to "The Plea" when she included it in *Lifted Masks and Other Works*, her collection of stories published in 1912.

"In the Face of His Constituents" was widely praised. The *Davenport Morning Star* complimented its fluid and polished style, while the *Palladium-Item* in Richmond, Indiana, called it a compelling work that appealed to the emotions of its readers and left them with a "haunting memory." The *Evening Times-Republican* in Marshalltown, Iowa, admired its "psychological insight," and ranked Glaspell as one of Iowa's top magazine writers.

Although the story is fictional, many Iowa residents in 1903 would have recognized it as inspired by the case of Wesley Elkins. The central character's background is nearly identical to Wesley's, and several of the most dramatic speeches and scenes are adapted from those on the floor of the state legislature in 1902.

Iowa newspapers alerted their readers to the connection and recalled the facts of the case. Glaspell had depicted her central character in the most sympathetic terms, focusing on his remarkable transformation in prison, and reporters followed her lead. The *Chariton Patriot*, for example, ran an article under the headline "A STORY FOR IOWA PEOPLE: IOWA LEGISLATURE INCIDENT IS MATERIAL FOR STORY IN HARPER'S." It emphasized how the boy in Glaspell's story, like Wesley Elkins, "was a most exemplary convict and made wonderful progress in learning, especially along literary lines," and whose petitions to the legislature were "models of good composition and strong writing."

Susan Glaspell was twenty-seven years old in 1903 when "In the Face of His Constituents" was published. After graduating from Drake University, she had worked as a reporter in Des Moines, initially covering the legislature. In 1902, she was assigned to a criminal trial, a case that would later inspire her classic works: the play, "Trifles," written in 1916, and the short story, "A Jury of Her Peers," in 1917. She had not yet made her mark in 1903. She had moved back to her hometown of Davenport, Iowa, declaring that she would devote herself to writing fiction.

"In the Face of His Constituents" was the first piece Glaspell placed in such a well-respected publication as *Harper's*. Under the editorship of Henry Mills Alden and William Dean Howells, the magazine prided itself on having a literate and serious readership, publishing fiction by celebrated authors, including Mark Twain, Edith Wharton, Stephen Crane, and Willa Cather. It sold more than 100,000 copies a month, and newspapers throughout the country, from Maine to California, publicized the stories and authors featured in each issue. Having a piece accepted by *Harper's* was an achievement for any writer, and especially for one as young as Glaspell.

The story is told from the internal perspective of a single character, Senator Harrison, who is forced to make a difficult moral decision. The legislature is debating a pardon for a young man who was a child when he committed his crime. Senator Harrison initially opposes the action, justifying his decision on objective principles. Glaspell relates the arguments from the other side as he listens to them, and readers are privy to the emotional reflections that gradually lead him to change his mind. He remembers himself as an eleven-year-old child, how he had often acted impulsively without thinking of the consequences. The influence of others had shaped his character, but what of a child who grew up without that? Was such a young child capable of forming a criminal intent, or were the hard circumstances of his early life to blame?

Four years earlier, in 1899, Glaspell had raised these same questions in her newspaper column about the riot at the girls' reform school in Mitchellville, Iowa. In the wake of the riot, some commentators attributed the girls' behavior to their unnatural and fixed characters. Others, including Glaspell, focused on the conditions of their lives as the cause, suggesting that these young girls could be rehabilitated under the right environment.

Glaspell knew that reformers had been raising these issues for years. In 1900, one year after Mitchellville, she was in Des Moines to report on the annual convention of the National Congress of Mothers, an organization formed to focus on child welfare. She listened as leaders of the group gave powerful speeches demanding juvenile justice reform, emphasizing the importance of parental guidance and proper care to a child's development. Children, they said, lacked the mental capacity of adults and should be treated differently. The law should consider the difficulties they faced in their early lives and their vulnerability to negative outside influences. Given education and spiritual instruction, young offenders offered the promise of rehabilitation and the most potential to be able to rejoin society.

In 1903, Glaspell added her voice to this reform movement. Throughout the spring of 1902, she had closely followed the legislative debate over Wesley Elkins' parole in the Des Moines newspapers. The articles reprinted many of the speeches in their entirety, with supporters making the same arguments endorsed by crusaders for juvenile justice reform. When Glaspell wrote her story, these ideals were in the forefront of her mind. Recreating the debate as fiction offered her the opportunity to advocate for these goals to a broader audience.

"In the Face of His Constituents" takes place on the floor of the state Senate, as legislators are deciding whether Alfred Williams, a young man modeled after Wesley Elkins, should be released from prison. When the story opens, Senator Harrison has just finished his speech opposing the pardon. He focused on a reasonable premise: that his constituents, who lived in the county where the crime had been committed, were entitled to make the judgment in this case, so that their united opposition should be determinative. Harrison prides himself as taking a stand that rises above personal feelings or sympathy: "the incarnation of outraged justice attempting to hold its own at the floodgates of emotion."

Harrison sits down to listen to the case made by Senator Dorman, a strong supporter of the young man. The rest of the narrative moves back and forth between outside reality—the words Harrison hears—and his inner thoughts and memories. Dorman starts by relating the facts of the case. Alfred is a young man in his early twenties who has spent twelve years in prison for killing his father and stepmother when he was a child of eleven years old. The brief description of Alfred's early life is taken from the saddest facts of Wesley's life: the divorce of his parents; his mother's death; his return to his father's house; and the neglect and mistreatment he suffered there. Dorman admits that Alfred committed a terrible crime, but he does not describe it in detail. Instead, he appeals to the emotions of his colleagues, seeking to convey the pain and hopelessness of the child, without a friend in the world or "some human being there to lay a cooling hand on his hot forehead, and say a few soothing, loving words to take the sting from the loneliness, and ease the suffering."

Dorman's story of Alfred's childhood is brief but evocative, and he follows with a description of the next twelve years. Alfred was sent to the penitentiary, and Dorman tells "of how he had expanded under kindness, of his wonderful mental attainments, the letters he could write, the books he had read, the hopes he had cherished." According to Dorman, the boy's transformation was the strongest evidence that he was not a born criminal.

Although Dorman describes the environment that shaped Alfred, his central point is the boy's age when he committed the crime, arguing that an eleven-year-old child is too young to be held criminally responsible, that he had acted out of "childish passion" rather than with criminal intent. Glaspell recreates an event from the legislative debate in Iowa when she has Dorman point to a young and innocent-looking page who is distributing papers among the senators. Dorman lifts the child to his desk and asks: "If this little fellow should be guilty of a like crime tonight, to what extent would you, in reading of it in the morning, charge him with the moral discernment which is the first condition of moral responsibility?"

As Senator Harrison listens, he sees that the argument is more logical than he had thought; Alfred's dramatic progress in prison seemed to prove that he was redeemable. The visual image of the young page triggers emotional memories for Harrison. An eleven-year-old child, he thinks, is more immature than he had imagined. He remembers his own recklessness when he was eleven, once throwing a rock at a schoolmate who teased him. In his case, he had learned to check his impulses, thanks to the guidance and encouragement of others.

Recollections from his boyhood convey to Harrison a powerful sense of what Alfred has lost: Alfred had never gone swimming, never attended a ball game or a circus, never owned a dog. As Harrison considers how he might have responded to the provocations in the boy's life, he realizes that circumstances—and not an innate criminal instinct—might have led even him to commit the crime.

Harrison comes to see Alfred as a victim—robbed of his childhood and then locked away in a dark cell—and he changes his mind about the pardon. He does not act immediately, and Glaspell recreates the drama on the floor of the Iowa legislature in 1902. In Glaspell's short story, the pardon is defeated on the first vote, with Harrison joining the majority. Immediately thereafter, and, to the surprise of the other legislators, he asks for reconsideration. A second roll call is taken, and Harrison reverses his position. That action persuades other senators to do so as well, and the motion to release Alfred is overwhelmingly approved.

Most people outside of Iowa who read "In the Face of His Constituents" in 1903, or "The Plea" as it was entitled in later years, would not have known that Alfred Williams was modeled on Wesley Elkins. Glaspell's intention was not to publicize Wesley's case. Instead, she structured her fictional work to highlight the beliefs that had inspired Wesley's supporters. As Senator Harrison is persuaded to change his mind, she encourages readers to see that children, even those who committed the worst crimes, could mature into responsible adults. She suggests that Alfred Williams—a young man who had committed his crime as a child—deserved a second chance. That he was deserving of that second chance was, of course, what Wesley was determined to prove.

Did Wesley read Glaspell's story? If so, he never mentioned it to the governor or to Professor Harlan.

26.

THE BEGINNING OF THE spring semester in 1904 was difficult for Wesley. He had dropped his English course, replacing it with Mathematics, but he was determined to study English texts and Civics on his own. In the evenings, he read the historical and political essays of Lord Thomas Macaulay, often staying up until midnight. He also had responsibilities to the Gladstone Society, and he was involved with the school newspaper, the *Cornellian*. Otis Moore, a classmate and editor-in-chief of the paper, was a friend, and Wesley wrote several of his monthly letters to the governor on the paper's masthead.

Wesley had had trouble with his eyes during his time at Anamosa. A doctor there had advised him to stop reading so much and had prescribed glasses for Wesley to wear for a time. In March 1904, Wesley reported to Governor Cummins that he feared his eyesight was getting worse, making studying difficult at times. Wesley understood that he would have to take a lighter load and get more sleep in order to continue in school.

Wesley felt better as the spring semester progressed. As always, he worried about his expenses. Although he found it difficult to hold a paying job while taking classes, he earned some money working in the registrar's office at the end of the semester. He did not want to incur more debt or depend on help from others, and he contemplated taking a semester off to earn money.

In June 1904, and with the governor's consent, Wesley boarded the train to make another trip to Blooming Prairie. He had begun to think about moving to a city in Minnesota where he could save the cost of tuition by going to a public school. If he could find part-time jobs in a city, he hoped he could save enough to return to Cornell.

As it turned out, his letter in June 1904—number 27 out of 122—would be the last he would write from Iowa.

Wesley arrived at Cora Bassett's farm in Blooming Prairie on June 27. In July, he reported to Governor Cummins: "I have been out in the open air constantly since the close of school and am almost as brown as an Indian. Am feeling pretty good and I think my eyes are a bit better and will in time be seeing as ever."

In August 1904, Wesley traveled by bicycle the seventy-five miles from Blooming Prairie to St. Paul, Minnesota, finding places to stay overnight along his route. He was on his trip on the evening of August 20, when a freak storm tore through the northern Midwest.

The storm began to form in South Dakota a few days earlier. The skies darkened, and the winds howled. Thunderstorms let loose torrential rains. In the town of Willow Lake, three churches, most of the wood frame houses, a school, grain elevators, and livery barns were reduced to rubble. Seventeen box cars on a rail siding were tossed in the air like toys. The Methodist church flipped over and landed on the parsonage. A newspaper report claimed that "every building was wrecked."

Continuing eastward, the storm created a path of destruction across southern Minnesota that devastated communities, killing fourteen individuals and injuring more than 200. Called a tornado by some observers and a cyclone by others, the storm ripped into St. Paul around 8:30 P.M. on August 20. Sections of the High Bridge over the Mississippi River were destroyed. Damage was heaviest in the downtown, near the Wabasha Street Bridge. The storm caused a panic among patrons at the Tivoli Concert Hall and the Empire Theatre when the buildings began to shake and the roofs were torn off.

The U.S. Weather Bureau anemometer on top of the *Pioneer*

Press building was wrenched from its mountings after registering winds of 110 miles per hour, with gusts up to 180 miles per hour. Most of the windows in the building were blown out. Wesley was a few days late in writing his letter in August, delaying until he reached St. Paul after the storm had passed. He must have taken shelter somewhere during his journey, and he would have witnessed the destruction in the city when he arrived. In his letter to the governor, however, he didn't mention what he had been through or what he had seen. He wrote:

> I have been working in the harvest field quite steady lately and it was such heavy work that it almost used me up so I thought I would take a trip up here on a wheel and canvass for the National Magazine on the way so as to pay expenses. . . . I can return by another road and then pay expenses back. I have been getting all the work I could so to pay up my debt at Mt. Vernon. I have paid up the most pressing ones, but owe the college about $30.00 yet. I hope to get everything paid up soon for I don't like to owe anything.

SHORTLY AFTER arriving in St. Paul, Wesley made the difficult decision to ask the governor if he could move there. He was conflicted about leaving Mount Vernon: he had friends at Cornell, and he had taken on responsibilities for the Gladstone Society. Yet, as he told the governor, he didn't see how he could afford to return. While another year at Cornell would only increase his substantial debt, he could continue his education in St. Paul without the cost of tuition. Employment opportunities were bound to be greater in the city, so he expected that he could earn enough to support himself while also gradually paying off what he owed.

Wesley knew that the move to St. Paul would be challenging. He wrote to the governor that "the coming year will be a test for myself whether I have the grit and determination sufficient to carry me through the school year and make all personal expenses. I am willing to do any honest work that will help me to continue in school." While in prison, Wesley had aspired to be educated and well-read. Now that he had been released from prison, Wesley focused on another goal, one that had gradually become more important to him and that would motivate him for the rest of his life: he wanted to be independent and provide for himself.

Governor Cummins gave his consent to the move in early September 1904. Wesley responded gratefully a few days later. He noted that he was glad that Professor Harlan had been consulted for "I know of no man whom I have learned to love so dearly as Prof. Harlan." Now that he was alone in a new place, he asked the governor for help in finding employment, writing "I would also be very glad to meet any one in St. Paul whom you know and explain what I am trying to do for myself."

Wesley found lodging at a five-story residential hotel called The Angus and arranged to work there as payment for room and board. The Angus was a splendid building, featuring elaborate exterior brick work, a rounded tower at the northeastern corner, and pressed metal decorative work at the top. Three-sided gothic oriel windows projected from the upper floors.

Wesley had modest accommodations, probably a single sleeping room and shared bath. Situated at the corner of Selby and Western Avenues, the hotel was just four blocks north of Summit Avenue and only a few steps from a streetcar stop. Since Wesley would need to take public transportation, the location was ideal.

Soon after arriving in the city, Wesley enrolled in Central High School, the oldest high school in Minnesota and the largest in St. Paul. All the public schools in St. Paul were crowded, and in 1904, the student population at Central was more than 1,200. The three-story brick structure located at Tenth and Minnesota Streets occupied most of a full city block and was defined by an impressive tower on one corner and an astronomical observatory with a fixed telescope on another corner. The school's debate society had raised the money to cover the cost of the observatory. The building had over forty classrooms and served more than twice the number of students enrolled at Cornell.

On September 19, 1904, Wesley provided an update to Governor Cummins:

> I entered Central High School here at the opening of the fall term. I like the school though I would prefer to be at Cornell, and I am still entertaining the thought of finishing at Cornell.
> . . . I like my work at The Angus, but it interferes a good deal with my school work. From 4 P.M. to 10 P.M. there is practically no opportunity to study. I hope, however, to make a success of the year. I hope to secure a morning newspaper route. If I do, it will pay from $14.00 to $20.00 per month for about one hours work each morning.

WHEN WESLEY settled in St. Paul, the population was close to 200,000. The city was larger than Los Angeles, Salt Lake City, Seattle, or Denver. The combined population of St. Paul and Minneapolis made the Twin Cities the eighth most populous urban area in the country. If Wesley wanted a place where he might live without being noticed, St. Paul was a good choice.

The city's most famous resident was a successful businessman named James J. Hill. Born in Ontario, Canada, he had moved to St. Paul in 1855 when he was seventeen. He was short, blind in his right eye due to a bow-and-arrow accident, and bursting with energy and ambition.

Hill started out as a bookkeeper for a steamship company, quickly learning how the transportation industry worked and how commodities were moved from one location to another by boat and rail. By his late twenties, he had started or engaged in several entrepreneurial ventures, and eventually enticed other investors to join with him in purchasing railroads. By the late 1880s under his ownership, Hill had merged several railroads into a single entity called the Great Northern Railway. Known as the "Empire Builder," Hill was one of the wealthiest men of his generation, the so-called Robber Barons of the Gilded Age.

One day in the future, Wesley would find employment in the railroad industry that was dominated by men like James Hill. In 1904, however, Wesley was focused primarily on making a living and going to school. Although The Angus was a convenient location for Wesley, he decided to move. In October, he reported to Governor Cummins:

> I am looking after the steam heating plant in the Harlan Flats, a three-story brick building, and doing such other work as may be required. I do not average at the most more than three hours per day and I get the same as I did at The Angus, my board and room.

AS HE HAD HOPED, Wesley was able to get a paper route, delivering the morning edition of the *Pioneer Press* to nearly one hundred customers. In order to be hired for the job, he had to post a $100 bond. He didn't have the money, but he availed himself of a Cornell College connection, asking Pastor Samuel G. Smith of the People's Church of St. Paul to sign for the bond. Smith was a Cornell College graduate, and Wesley had met him after Smith gave a lecture at the college in the fall of 1902. Pastor Smith agreed to sign the bond for Wesley's route.

Wesley had to get up at 4:30 A.M. to pick up his papers and start his delivery route. He began his day before dawn, returned to Harlan Flats by 6:30 A.M. to get the furnace going, and then rushed to catch the streetcar to Central High for his first class.

He was now living in a city where his past and name were unknown, and he was eager to remain anonymous. In his October letter to Governor Cummins, Wesley wrote that he was "studiously avoiding everything, in school and out, that would tend to bring my name before the public. Thus far no St. Paul paper has mentioned my being in the city, and I certainly hope they will remain ignorant of my presence."

BEFORE LONG St. Paul was plunged into the depths of winter. Although Wesley had experienced snow and harsh conditions in Iowa, the Minnesota winter was longer and the cold more penetrating. Under bright blue skies, St. Paul was a frozen city from December until early spring. Banks of snow rose alongside streets and sidewalks and then crusted with ice and firmed up, solid as boulders. Icicles hung like daggers from the edges of houses and buildings. Light poles were slick with ice. Horses exhaled plumes of warm air as they trudged through the frigid streets.

Wesley was out in the brittle air to deliver his papers before the sun rose, and he was sleeping just five hours a night. As would continue to be the case, he was concerned about his finances. He wasn't sure he could stay in school, cover his own expenses, and pay off his debt.

By December, Wesley had found a temporary solution. He moved once again, and he waited tables at breakfast and dinner, paying for his board while spending less time at the job. By keeping his paper route, he would earn enough money to send some to Cornell. At the same time, Wesley was making good progress at Central. Based on his examination results, his English teacher had recommended that Wesley be advanced a half year ahead of the rest of his class.

In the early months of 1905, Wesley seemed to relax in the new environment. He admitted to the governor that he had felt very unsettled in St. Paul at first and was now feeling more comfortable. In March, he wrote: "Everything has kept swinging in about the same old way since I wrote my last letter."

Wesley was particularly pleased about his job with the *Pioneer Press*. In early May, a competing newspaper, the *St. Paul Globe*, had gone out of business, and the *Press* offered a competition to determine which carrier could register the most first-time sub-scribers. It took 160 points to win, and Wesley easily beat out the others with 204 points. His employer rewarded him with a gold watch. By June, Wesley had 170 subscribers on his route and was earning $34.00 a month, nearly double what he had hoped.

When the school year ended, Wesley found a job "firing a hot water plant." He kept at his newspaper route, taking only a ten-day break in August to visit his sister in Blooming Prairie. His vacation was shorter than usual, and the time passed quickly. In addition, he had had to pay two substitutes to take over the route, and neither one had performed as well as Wesley. He wrote that "it was quite a pleasure for me to receive the welcome back that I received. It convinced me the more fully that efforts to please and give satisfaction to one's employer are not entirely without satisfaction."

In September 1905, he began his second year at Central High School, reporting to the governor that he was "again in the har-ness." He registered as a junior for five classes: Algebra, Latin, Modern History, and two in English. He continued to rise at 4:30 A.M. for his paper route, and, despite his busy schedule, he involved himself in school activities.

Wesley joined the debate society at Central that fall. After excel-ling in a contest held in his English class, he was chosen out of a group of fifty students to be president and officer at the debates for the term.

Two months later, in November, he reported to the governor that he was continuing to advance: "I took part in one debate, presided at two others, was chairman of a committee to draw up a constitution for a new debating society, and am on our Assem-bly debate for next Monday. I have worked seventeen hours out of twenty-four."

In early December of 1905, he was elected to compete in the Junior–Senior Annual Debate scheduled for January. It was an honor, he told the governor, but he was apprehensive about the time commitment.

In mid-December, Wesley received a letter from Professor Harlan, and he wrote a long response to him a few weeks later, including a dizzying list of new responsibilities:

At a meeting of the Board of Directors of *The World*—our high school newspaper—yesterday I was elected Exchange Editor for 1906.

In addition to all this, I am president of the 4th English class, member of the Rhetoric class debating committee, chairman of the Program Committee of the Debate Club and Chairman of the Junior–Senior joint committee on debates.

Wesley's letter closed with this paragraph:

The Clayton County paper is mistaken about where I am and what I am doing. I have been in Minneapolis a great many times for one reason or another but I haven't worked there, nor have I done any stenographic work since I came to St. Paul.

Professor Harlan must have sent Wesley a brief article that had appeared in the *Elkader Argus* in November. The newspaper told its readers that it had learned the whereabouts of Wesley Elkins, reminding readers that he was the eleven-year-old boy who had murdered his parents and was sentenced to life in prison. The paper claimed incorrectly that Wesley had been "pardoned" by the legislature four years earlier and had "mastered shorthand and typewriting and now holds a good position in this line of work in Minneapolis."

No editorial comment accompanied the article, and there was no mention that people in Clayton County might still view Wesley as a threat to society. Wesley must have feared, though, that the overwhelming hostility toward him had not entirely dissipated. He would have seen the article as a warning; the facts were wrong, but it suggested that those who knew his background might still find him.

Over the next six months, during the spring and early summer of 1906, Wesley grew increasingly anxious that his past might be

exposed. Hard-won accomplishments and honors meant publicity, and Wesley wondered if the benefits were worth that cost.

Although Wesley did not want to attract attention in St. Paul, he
did not hide from people who already knew his story. Throughout
his years in Iowa and Minnesota, Wesley made several trips to
legislators who had spoken in his favor, including Senator Whipple, one of Wesley's strongest advocates, who invited Wesley to
stay with him and his family for several days. Wesley accepted
invitations from other supporters in Iowa, and he made a special
trip to see Warden Madden. Once he moved to Minnesota, he and
Professor Harlan visited back and forth several times.

Wesley stayed in touch with former classmates, and he kept
up with activities at the college. He had enjoyed the collegiality
of Cornell, and he wished he could have continued there. In a
letter to Professor Harlan in August, Wesley noted that several of
his friends were leaving St. Paul to continue their education. He
would particularly miss Otis Moore, the former editor-in-chief of
the *Cornellian*, who was moving to New York to enter Columbia.
Another was returning to Mount Vernon to resume his education
at Cornell. Wesley had not graduated from Central High School,
but he was curious about the college curriculum, and he asked
Professor Harlan to send him a catalog of courses. He added
that he was closely following the school's debate team. He wrote,
"I was very much surprised at the result of the Cornell–Carleton
debate this spring. I had a long talk with Harry Shaw when he was
in the city looking up the debate question. I felt quite certain that
Cornell would win that debate."

Ada Miller was another friend of Wesley's from Cornell. By 1905,
she had begun her studies at the Los Angeles Normal School, later
to become UCLA, where she would earn a PhD and go on to have
a career as a teacher. In a letter to Professor Harlan, she wrote
that she had corresponded with Wesley. She didn't know many
details, although she felt "sure that he is doing well, whatever his
work." A few months later, she reported to Harlan that she had

heard again from Wesley, and she added, "What a joy it is to see him doing so well. It is so right that he should have a chance to redeem his life—and I believe he is doing this nobly."

BEFORE THE spring semester of 1906 ended, Wesley received another significant honor: he was elected president of the State Oratorical Society of Minnesota. In May, stationery was printed under the Society's letterhead, featuring the names and schools of all the officers. The vice president and other officers were men from high schools across the state. The first entry in the list, which would be distributed throughout the state, read "President: Wesley Elkins, Central High School, St. Paul."

After accepting the position, Wesley had second thoughts, and he wrote to the governor that "I may resign, for the reason that my past history seems to be unknown here or forgotten. It doesn't seem just right to accept this position under the circumstances, and I want nothing to happen that would bring my past before the public."

Cummins must have cautioned Wesley against stepping down. Wesley responded, agreeing that it might attract attention and writing, "It is undoubtedly true that a resignation without a good reason would cause considerable comment."

Wesley wanted to stay in school. He was involved in activities and committed to take on responsibilities. His classmates were bound to be disappointed if he left, and yet he had begun to weigh his other options.

IN JUNE OF 1906, Wesley accepted a summer job in the office of the General Superintendent of the Omaha Road, a railway company operating in the upper Midwest, connecting Chicago, Omaha, St. Paul, Minneapolis, and various small cities of the region. Keeping up his paper route in the early mornings gave him little time for anything except work, and he had to forgo his trip to visit Cora in Blooming Prairie. He still hoped to graduate—either from Cornell Academy or Central High School—but he wasn't sure that was practical. His job provided him with the anonymity and the steady flow of income he desired.

In August 1906, Wesley wrote a long letter to Professor Harlan, and it was clear that Wesley was serious about his employment prospects with the railroad. He wasn't certain whether he should stay with the Omaha Road or consider moving to the Minneapolis office of the Milwaukee line. He wondered if Harlan had friends who knew more about the Milwaukee line. The railroad industry was growing rapidly, and Wesley was proud of its success. He wrote:

> Next week will be a very busy one for the railroads, as the state fair opens on the 4th of September. The state fair board promises one of the greatest fairs ever held in Minnesota, but this, I believe, is what is promised each year. Several events in the past month or two have taxed the railroads to the utmost. A week or so since we had the National G.A.R. Encampment at Minneapolis which brought about 60,000 to 70,000 visitors to the Twin Cities. About the first of the month St. Paul had the Northwestern Saengerfest, which brought thousands into the city. In addition to these, several minor conventions were held in St. Paul which gave the roads all they could do.

IN SEPTEMBER 1906, Wesley made his decision: his future was more secure if he stayed where he was, seeking to advance with the Omaha Road. Explaining his choice, he told the governor:

> In a railroad office, as in other business, one cannot be jumping around here and there, dipping in this and dipping in that. So I have decided that for the present at least I would remain in this office and attend night school and take up such particular work as I most need.

Although Wesley had been absorbed in his education for years, he was now choosing to give that up, leaving before graduation.

He didn't explain to the governor what he told his classmates, or how he justified resigning from his much-publicized leadership positions. Perhaps it was enough to say that he was choosing to enter the workforce. Although he had told the governor that he might enroll in night school, he would never again register for classes.

The formal education of Wesley Elkins had come to an end.

27.

WESLEY STARTED WORK with the Omaha Road in June 1906, and a month later, he turned twenty-eight years of age. He did not know it yet, but he had found his niche. Wesley was about to become part of the greatest and most flourishing industry of the era.

In one of his first debates at Cornell, Wesley had argued on the issue of tariffs, so it's likely that he had researched and studied the history of the railroad industry. As the country's population moved westward, the development of the railroads in the mid-nineteenth century impacted travel and commerce. The challenge was to figure out how to link the two coasts and reduce the time and cost of travel for people and goods.

When President Abraham Lincoln signed into law the Pacific Railroad Act of 1862, the legislation set in motion the construction of what was to be known as the transcontinental railroad, linking the tracks of the Central Pacific Railroad with the tracks of the Union Pacific Railroad. It would be an engineering and entrepreneurial success of the highest order, the greatest American technological accomplishment of the nineteenth century.

The actual physical building of the route—surveying, designing, constructing—took more than five years of steady work. The tracks were joined at Promontory Summit in Utah on May 10, 1869. Leland Stanford—an ex-governor of California, a future U.S. Senator, and one of the four founding partners of the Central Pacific—struck the blow that officially joined the two sets of tracks, driving a golden spike into a pre-drilled hole.

The age of transcontinental travel and commerce had begun. Fortunes would be made and lost as the railroads and business speculators strategized to take advantage of this new technology.

Politics and business had merged. Corruption would follow. For cities like St. Paul, soon to be the third largest rail center in the country, it meant that employees of the railroads were on the ground floor of an industry that was destined to become the cornerstone of the national economy for years to come.

AFTER WESLEY accepted full-time employment with the railroad, he reported to the governor that his work was "steady and exacting. Mistakes will not be tolerated." In his mind, the position held great potential and the promise of security.

In November 1906, Wesley moved again, this time to room with a friend from Central High School. His new residence was more than four miles from his office, but it was near the campus of Hamline University. Although it was inconvenient to live farther away, the Hamline area was quiet and beautiful in the summer.

Six months later, in May 1907, Wesley was transferred to the Comptroller's Office. He was now making fifty dollars a month and had new and difficult responsibilities that he described in some detail to Governor Cummins:

> I am working in 'Train Earnings'—new work made necessary by new laws. We handle all the numerous forms of tickets handled by conductors on the entire system, figure out the mileage of each passenger on our main and branch line trains and figure out the earnings of each train according to the local and interstate rates. As the rates are different in the several states, it makes quite a mix up in tariffs, especially as we must follow each passenger to the end of his journey or until he leaves our line. Sometimes he may be on two or three trains. In that case we must credit each train with the number of miles the passenger rode on it. All fares of tickets are separated and figured by their respective rates.

Employees of the Omaha Road could ride free on the passenger trains, and Wesley took advantage of his rail pass to travel without being constrained by costs. In the summer of 1907, he took a longer vacation than usual, traveling with several friends to Lake Okoboji in northwestern Iowa. At the end of the trip, he looped back east to stay with his sister, Cora, in Blooming Prairie.

In August 1907, Wesley made another major change in his life. After fourteen months at the Omaha Road, he accepted a position with the Northern Pacific Railway in the Office of the Auditor of Disbursements. His starting monthly salary would be fifty dollars, and he thought he could advance more quickly than with the Omaha. As always, Wesley was looking ahead: he wrote to the governor that the new job would give him the chance to work with the Interstate Commerce Act, and "experienced voucher men are in demand by all roads."

Considering the fact that the national economy was in a severe downturn—the stock market declined by twenty-five percent during the first nine months of 1907, a recessionary move that impacted the value of railroad stocks—it was a bold move on Wesley's part to be switching employers at this time. Two months after Wesley changed jobs, the country experienced the Panic of 1907. Wesley felt sure that his job was secure even though "all the roads have let off a great many men and cut salaries unmercifully." He reported that he had more than enough work to keep him busy, and soon after he started his new job, his salary was raised to sixty dollars a month. Three months later, he would be earning sixty-five dollars a month, and, a year after that, his monthly salary would be raised again to seventy-five dollars.

THE NORTHERN PACIFIC had its own twisted history. Chartered by the U.S. Congress in 1864, the path of the Northern Pacific would take it across the Dakota Territory, some of the most desolate and unsettled land in the northern plains. Due to various issues of financing and resources, the project was not completed until 1883 when a second golden spike was hammered into the tracks at Gold Creek, Montana.

Around the same time that the Northern Pacific was being completed, James Hill was building a parallel route from St. Paul, westward to the Pacific. In the two decades before Wesley came to work for the Northern Pacific Railway, the railroad industry experienced growing pains and vital setbacks: bankruptcies, litigation, and changes in ownership. Hill had tried to seize control of the Northern Pacific, forming a trust that was eventually broken up by President Theodore Roosevelt and the 1904 Supreme Court decision *Northern Securities Co. v. United States.*

Wesley's position in the Office of the Auditor of Disbursements offered him perspective on the railroad industry, its finances and increasing power. He knew that influential men, such as James Hill and J. P. Morgan, ultimately controlled the destiny of the industry. Some railroads would die or be absorbed; others would survive and thrive. Despite the ruling in *Northern Securities*, the managements of various rail lines continued to work together to promote their common interests.

In the late 1890s, the Northern Pacific upgraded its equipment and service, utilizing larger and more powerful steam locomotives. The North Coast Limited was quickly acknowledged to be one of the finest passenger trains in the country, known for its premier dining car service. Wesley had judged that the Northern Pacific would make it, and he was right. The Northern Pacific continued to operate as an independent railroad until 1970.

PERSONNEL FILES of the Northern Pacific are archived at the Minnesota State Historical Society. The file for Wesley Elkins is relatively thin, but it provides some pertinent information about his employment history. Most of the forms in his file were filled out and signed by his supervisors, who noted the regular increases in his salary.

The file includes basic biographical information collected over the years: name, address, nearest living relative, place and date of birth, nationality, weight, height, and the color of his eyes and hair. He was slightly built as an adult: five feet, three inches tall and 125 pounds. He had dark brown hair and blue eyes. One form that Wesley himself signed was dated May 1913. On this page, he listed his birthdate as July 12, 1879, one year later than he had claimed in the past. While that date conflicts with other records, it is less significant than another alteration of his history: Wesley stated on the form that he was born in Madison, Wisconsin. He knew that was not true. Changing the place of his birth made it harder for anyone in Minnesota to trace his history back to Iowa or link him to the crime in Clayton County.

FROM THE SUMMER of 1907 until the summer of 1908, Wesley's letters to the governor were brief, only one or two lines noting that he was pleased with his work. Sometimes, he mentioned he was suffering from health problems, likely caused by the difficult climate in St. Paul. In February, he reported that he "had a little touch of the grippe and catarrh trouble. This latter trouble I have each winter and I do not know as I will ever get any relief in this direction."

When his friend from Central High School graduated in the spring of 1908, Wesley moved to a rooming house at 51 Summit Avenue, near St. Paul's Cathedral in the heart of the city and closer to where he worked. From his room on Summit Avenue, he was only a five-minute walk from the James Hill mansion.

Wesley was thinking about more than his new neighborhood or his work. His schedule left little time to socialize or make new friends. He recalled how much he had enjoyed his visits to Blooming Prairie, spending time with Mark and Cora and their families, and he wanted to renew other connections from the past. It had been many years since he had left Waterloo, Iowa—he was seven when his birthmother, Matilda Blackwell, died, and now he was thirty—but he remembered with pleasure the time he had spent in that city with her and her second husband, William Dowden.

There had been three other children, now all adults: Will, who was six years older than Wesley; Georgianna, who was the same age as Wesley; and Elmer, who was blind and had been born to Wesley's mother and William Dowden the year before Wesley left.

While Wesley was at Anamosa, William and his children had moved from Iowa to Arkansas. We don't know the path they followed or the reason for their move. Census records, however, show that, by the summer of 1908, William had a home in Mammoth Spring, Arkansas, which he shared with his two younger children and a grandchild: his son, Elmer, now twenty-five; Georgianna, who was thirty; and Georgianna's seven-year-old daughter, Pearl. Georgianna was a widow whose husband, John Ellis, had died shortly after they were married in 1900, and just a few months before Pearl was born. Dowden's oldest child, Will, had relocated to South Dakota.

We don't know whether Wesley remained in touch with the Dowden family during his years at Anamosa. We know that he and his half-sister, Cora, exchanged letters, and it's possible that Wesley also communicated with the Dowdens. Although William Dowden, with three children of his own, sent seven-year-old Wesley back to Clayton County, Dowden had been fond of the boy who had lived with them for a few years. If William or Georgianna Dowden wrote letters to Wesley, none of them have survived in the archives. Wesley's letters to Governor Cummins reveal only that sometime after Wesley moved to St. Paul, he and William Dowden were in touch with each other, and that Dowden had invited him to his home in Arkansas.

Wesley would finally make that trip in the summer of 1908.

28.

IN JULY 1908, Wesley wrote to Governor Cummins to say that he hoped to travel south for a few days in August to visit the Dowden family. He had not seen them for more than twenty years, and he wrote, "I look forward to meeting them with considerable pleasure and with some curiosity as to how they have changed since we were little children together."

The next month, Wesley reported that his visit had been "exceedingly pleasant." He had already formed a special bond with young Pearl, who, he said, "thinks there is no one on earth like her Uncle Wesley." He also mentioned that William Dowden was thinking of selling his house. Wesley wrote to the governor that they "would like to relocate so we could all be together." William, at seventy-three, was retired, and Georgianna was not employed, and so their financial situation may well have been precarious. In contrast, Wesley had a steady source of income, and he was confident that he could stay well employed.

He and the Dowdens had already discussed where they might live, and Wesley wrote:

> They might come to St. Paul, but I think it would be to my best interests for me to go south or west. Something certainly must be done soon to give me relief from my catarrh trouble, which is now affecting my throat. While south I seemed relieved, which I suppose was due to the dry climate and by being out in the open air nearly all the time.
>
> Prof. Harlan seems to think Los Angeles would be a good place to go, but I do not like the idea of going so far away from all my relatives. . . . Nothing can be done at present, for the fall

is a poor time to change employment, but in the spring I would like to see what I can do with some southern road. With my experience in railway accounting offices, I anticipate but little trouble in locating elsewhere.

The Dowdens waited a year, until May of 1909, before making the move. Another place might have been better for his lungs, but Wesley decided it was more important to keep his job in St. Paul than to look for another.

As always with the colder weather, Wesley's health declined. Today his catarrh trouble would be diagnosed as a persistent infection of the lungs, and he continued to suffer from the condition through the fall and winter of 1908. His physical problems grew more severe in October when he contracted the flu and was bedridden for two weeks. Even after he returned to work, he continued to have chronic sinusitis and trouble breathing. Eventually he consulted a nose and throat specialist. The doctor gave him little hope of improving unless he moved to a milder climate, away from the bitter weather and the artificial heat of a closed office with little ventilation. And yet, as he anticipated the arrival of the Dowdens, Wesley wanted to stay where he was. He knew that his employer was pleased with his work, and he expected his salary to increase. He wanted to be sure that he could support his family.

The blistering cold of another Minnesota winter was difficult for Wesley. During the 1908 calendar year, St. Paul accumulated sixty-five inches of snow, the most since records were kept. Temperatures seldom rose above freezing. Many days the thermometer dipped below zero. The wind chill was brutal, and Wesley's health would not improve until the spring.

In February, Wesley was pleased to receive his promotion, and he was transferred to the railroad bill desk. He was given more responsibility and a higher salary, although his new duties required him to work longer hours, including many evenings. In March, he reported to the governor, "I have my new work lined up in pretty fair shape and in a couple of weeks I expect to have it right up to date. The greatest difficulty so far is balancing up the books. About a million and a half dollars in bills go into my books alone each month."

IN MAY 1909, the last vestiges of winter finally receded. Flowers bloomed and the Minnesota landscape turned green. People planted vegetable gardens. Thanks to the warmer weather, Wesley felt better by the time the Dowdens arrived on May 16. He reported the news to the governor with pleasure, noting that "My little eight-year-old niece says she will never go back to Arkansas now, but that she is going to stay with Uncle Wesley. As soon as we get things arranged, we expect to be pretty nicely located."

The reunion with these distant relatives offered Wesley a settled domestic and family life for the first time. Wesley rented a three-bedroom house on Jessamine Avenue and furnished it to accommodate four adults and the child, Pearl. The Dowdens arrived with some furniture and an organ they had owned in Arkansas. Wesley bought a piano. The house filled with music.

In his June letter to the governor, Wesley reported "I find a great difference between a boarding life and a home of one's own."

Although Wesley was always cautious with his money, he wanted to become a homeowner and thought he could afford a house costing $3,000. He was eager to be settled before the winter came, and after searching through the summer, he found what he wanted. Although the price of $3,350 was slightly more than he budgeted, the terms were reasonable, and he predicted that he could pay it off in ten years.

On October 26, 1909, Wesley signed the papers to purchase a newly built house at 1918 Ashland Avenue in Merriam Park, a growing residential area located midway between Minneapolis and St. Paul. His was the only name on the deed. The house had six rooms and a bathroom and stood on a narrow lot shaded by hardwood trees. A screen porch looked out over the backyard, which was well suited for a garden.

Now, just seven years after he left prison, Wesley entered a new phase of his life as the head of a household. In November, Wesley wrote to the governor that he was "anticipating the pleasure of eating Thanksgiving dinner in my own home." He continued to work in the accounting department of the Northern Pacific, and he earned enough to pay the bills for the family group of five. They fell into a comfortable routine. Every morning Wesley walked to the station where he caught the streetcar. Georgianna cooked and kept the house, and when Wesley returned from work, the five of them ate meals together at the dining room table.

Wesley took a special interest in Pearl. The young girl had been excited to enroll in the new school, and she and her "Uncle Wesley" grew close. He was concerned about Pearl's health when she contracted the measles and missed an entire month of classes. Although he worked many nights, Wesley set aside time to be with his family. He talked about his plans for a garden with Pearl and listened to her practice the piano.

In February 1910, Wesley was called for jury duty. Did the clerk of court know that he had served twelve years in prison for the crime of murder and would only be eligible for a pardon after two more years of good behavior? Wesley had not revealed those facts to his employer, and perhaps the clerk of court was not aware of his history. Wesley didn't provide any details to the governor about his jury service, reporting only that he had served for two weeks and had to work long hours at his office to make up for the time he missed.

Later that spring he and Pearl planted vegetables and flowerbeds in the backyard. As Wesley observed in his letter in May, "My garden is doing nicely, and I am expecting good things for the table soon. The little girl has a little garden of her own and is trying to beat me raising good things."

ALTHOUGH HE made it through another freezing Minnesota winter without a flare up of his symptoms, Wesley became seriously ill in early June 1910, first with pleurisy and then with pneumonia. He was sick for more than a month: he had trouble breathing and the left side of his body ached, making it difficult for him to sleep. Recognizing the seriousness of Wesley's condition, his employer arranged for him to be treated at the Northern Pacific Hospital in Brainerd, about 105 miles north of St. Paul.

Wesley rode the train from St. Paul to Brainerd on June 20. Brainerd had always been a railroad town, established in 1881 as the first headquarters of the Northern Pacific, and most residents worked for the company. Many patients at the hospital were railroad employees who were provided free medical care for illnesses or accidents.

When the train rolled to a stop at the hospital, Wesley got off and faced the main building. The hospital had been designed by the renowned Minnesota architect Cass Gilbert, who had previously designed the state capitol building in St. Paul. With three stories and three distinctive towers, the hospital was an imposing structure. A wide porch wrapped all the way around the front. The building looked like a fancy hotel.

Wesley was admitted and treated for the inflammation in his lungs. The next month, he reported to the governor that doctors had opened his left side and drained 32 ounces of fluid. When he returned home in early July, he continued to have trouble sleeping, and the pains on his left side persisted. Hoping that fresh air might ease his discomfort, he began sleeping in the back porch, which was screened and protected from rain.

He mentioned his physical condition in every letter to the governor from June 1910 through March 1911. His left side throbbed, and that side of his neck was stiff. He worried about becoming seriously ill once again in the winter.

BY THIS TIME, Wesley had sent over one hundred letters to the governor's office. For six and a half years, starting in May 1902, he had addressed them to Albert Cummins, the man who had signed his parole papers. Cummins had always wanted to go into national politics, and he achieved that goal in 1908 when he was elected as the next U.S. Senator from Iowa.

Starting in 1908, Wesley addressed his letters to Beryl Franklin Carroll, who took office in November of that year. Born in 1860, Carroll had been a livestock dealer, a teacher, and a newspaper publisher before going into politics. He was a member of the Iowa Senate from 1895 until 1898, so he was certainly aware of the story of Wesley Elkins and his bid for freedom. During all of 1909 and going forward, Wesley sent his monthly reports to Governor Carroll.

Wesley's letters were mostly a recitation of facts. He was most expressive in the letters about his reunions with family: his summers with Cora and Mark; his visit to the Dowdens; and their decision to move almost 900 miles from Arkansas to Minnesota to live with him. He was pleased to tell the governor that Professor Harlan had visited him so that he could show him the house and introduce him to his family group.

By 1911, Wesley enjoyed a steady pattern of work and domestic life. As usual, the winter was long, and he suffered from the infection in his lungs and a severe cold. As always, he was glad when temperatures began to rise, and this year he anticipated the spring for another reason. The ten years of his conditional parole were due to end in April 1912, and if all went well, Governor Carroll would grant him a full pardon.

As the time approached, Wesley grew increasingly concerned about publicity. He wrote to Professor Harlan saying that he hoped people in Clayton County and St. Paul would be kept ignorant of the official end of his parole. He continued, "This is a serious matter with me and the fear of the outcome takes away the pleasure of the pardon."

Governor Carroll and Professor Harlan understood and respected Wesley's feelings. On March 28, 1912, Governor Carroll sent two copies of the official pardon document to Professor

Harlan and asked that he deliver one copy to Wesley in person. The governor wrote:

> The time fixed by the Governor for his pardon is not yet quite up but I thought perhaps we could avoid some publicity by attending to the case at once. . . . There will be nothing given out from this office and we will ask you to transmit one copy to Wesley and the other to the clerk and leave it to you to see that neither of them gives anything to the papers in regard to the case. By this means we may be able to avoid any further publicity.

The clerk who was to receive the copy of the pardon papers worked for the district court in Clayton County. In 1912, the clerk was Max Bishop, son of Hiram Bishop, the former senator from Clayton County who had vigorously opposed Wesley's release. Hiram Bishop was still active in his community and would, no doubt, hear about the pardon from his son. Professor Harlan wrote to the governor and asked if Senator Newberry, who had succeeded Hiram Bishop, could deliver the document to Max Bishop. The senator, Harlan thought, would be better at breaking the news. The governor assented to Harlan's request.

PROFESSOR HARLAN traveled to St. Paul soon after he received the pardon papers and presented them to Wesley. A few days later, on April 6, Wesley wrote to the governor for the last time. He said that he appreciated that the governor had chosen Professor Harlan to hand him the document in person, and he thanked Governor Carroll for his interest and for his "efforts in suppressing newspaper announcements of my pardon."

Nine days later, on April 15, 1912—four days before the tenth anniversary of his release from Anamosa—Wesley wrote to Professor Harlan to express his deep gratitude for his constant support, and to emphasize again the hope that the pardon would not be publicized:

Possibly some slight notice in the Elkader papers might not attract the attention of the St. Paul papers, which I am chiefly concerned about, but any notice in these papers is liable to be enlarged upon by others in the state and then attract attention of the St. Paul papers. I thank you however, sincerely, for your efforts in this matter and I suppose we can only hope for the best.

WESLEY WAS fortunate that Senator Newberry agreed that the less attention paid to the pardon, the better it would be for all concerned. Newberry wanted to meet with Max and Hiram Bishop together, and he planned to urge both father and son to keep the news as quiet as possible. Newberry wrote to Professor Harlan, "I will do the best I can to prevail upon them to keep the matter out of the papers as you suggest. I am sincerely in hopes that this can be done." Newberry's letter to Harlan was dated April 27, more than three weeks after the papers had been delivered to Wesley. The senator added a postscript: "I intend to go over to Elkader this week but am not likely to do so now for a week or ten days." Senator Newberry was not in a hurry to make the trip.

As Wesley had wished, the pardon received little attention in Clayton County, with only a brief note in the local newspapers. Neighbors of John and Hattie Elkins had been convinced that Wesley would threaten them again, but Wesley had kept his promise to stay away for ten years. Residents of Clayton County did not expect to see him again.

William P. Whipple, the former legislator and chair of the Senate Committee on Penitentiaries and Pardons who had argued most strenuously for Wesley's freedom, learned of the pardon only indirectly. He read about it in the newspapers near the end of April, and he wrote to Professor Harlan: "I trust that [Wesley] will realize his fondest hopes and yet I have no doubt but what he will meet with disappointments. Such is the history of man."

WESLEY'S LETTER TO Professor Harlan on April 15, 1912, is the last written communication from him we found in the archives. One can only imagine his profound sense of relief that he had been officially forgiven for his crime.

For more than twenty-two years, from the moment that he, as a child, had killed his parents on the moonlit night of July 17, 1889, Wesley had been watched and judged. He had lived in an adult prison for twelve years; been the focus of public debate and scrutiny; and spent a decade under the supervision of the governor of Iowa.

Wesley had accomplished more than his strongest supporters might have expected. As a mature and trustworthy adult, he was educated and independent, able to support himself and his family. Even those who had opposed his parole in 1902 must have recognized that Wesley Elkins had lived up to the commitment he had made to the legislature then: to lead "a life upright in character, strong and thoughtful, gentlemanly always," and "to justify the judgment and faithful effort of my friends."

Now, at the age of thirty-three—more than two decades since the murders—Wesley was finally free. His plea had been answered, and his long ordeal had ended.

29.

WESLEY ELKINS lived for another forty-nine years. After the letters stopped in 1912, however, the public record is sketchy.

Wesley saw the world transformed through two world wars and the Great Depression. Women gained the right to vote. Government-initiated programs sought to improve the education, health, and economic well-being of children, and to provide help for parents and pregnant women. In 1954, in *Brown v. Board of Education,* the Supreme Court ruled unanimously that segregation in public schools was unconstitutional, ushering in a new era of Civil Rights.

The swift pace of change would have been impossible to imagine by a boy born in 1878. In the second half of the twentieth century, Americans were linked as never before by means of modern communication, first by the telephone, then by the radio, and finally through the television set. The Golden Age of the movies came and went. While the railroads continued to be an important means of mass transportation, the great technological invention of the century was the airplane. If Wesley listened to President John F. Kennedy's inauguration in 1961, broadcast to the nation just a few months before Wesley died, he would have heard the young president predict that, by the end of the decade, America would send a manned spaceship to the moon, land it safely, and return it to earth.

Here is what we know about Wesley's life after 1912.

He remained in St. Paul, living in the house on Ashland Avenue, until the end of 1920. He continued to work for the Northern Pacific Railway Company and to support the family that he had brought together. In 1912, less than two months after his last letter to Governor Carroll, Wesley's blind half-brother, Elmer, died of tuberculosis in the Faribault State Hospital. Elmer Ellsworth Dowden, twenty-nine years old, was buried on June 1, 1912, in the hospital's cemetery.

Nearly four years later, heart disease claimed the life of William Dowden; he died on January 25, 1916, at the age of seventy-seven. William Dowden—the father figure in Wesley's life—was buried at Lakewood Cemetery in Minneapolis.

The family group was reduced to three: Wesley, Georgianna, and Pearl. In the fall of 1918, when the country entered World War I, Wesley registered for the draft. On his draft card, he described himself as being of medium height and having a medium build. The war ended before he was called into service.

Pearl had matured into a young woman, and she found a job. In 1920, the St. Paul City Directory lists her as a bookkeeper with the Omaha Road, the same company where her Uncle Wesley had first been employed.

When Wesley bought his house in the fall of 1909, he had calculated that he would own it free and clear in ten years. His prediction was off by only six months, and land records show that he made his last payment and became the owner of record in May 1920. A few days later, he transferred the title to Georgianna in exchange for one dollar of consideration.

That summer, Wesley turned forty-two years old. Most Americans aspired to purchase their own homes and live independently, and Wesley—thanks to his hard work and determination—had achieved that dream. Despite his persistent health problems, he had survived sixteen winters in one of the coldest states in the country. He had held a steady job for many years. He had maintained close relationships with some of his most ardent supporters, including Professor Harlan, who had encouraged Wesley for so long.

For years, Wesley had been advised by doctors that a warmer climate would improve his poor health, and he had often considered relocating to a southern state or to California. He had willingly accepted the financial responsibility for a family, and now they no longer had to depend on him. Pearl was employed, and Georgianna, as the owner of the house, was financially secure. Wesley was ready to make another major change.

Wesley resigned his position with the Northern Pacific Railway Company, effective December 31, 1920. He had worked with the company for thirteen years and had been rewarded by his employer with regular pay raises. His monthly salary had increased from $50 to $105, and his employee record was spotless. Nothing in his personnel file suggests that he was unhappy or dissatisfied with his work assignment.

Nevertheless, he left his job and the life he had so carefully created for himself in Minnesota.

WE DISCOVERED no records tracing Wesley's exact path after he left St. Paul, but we know that he traveled west and eventually settled in Hawaii. Wesley must have taken the train to the West Coast, and perhaps he followed the route that was later made famous by the Empire Builder, the passenger train named in honor of James Hill. The trip would have taken Wesley across the broad plains of North Dakota, through Montana and Glacier National Park, and then on to either Portland or Seattle. From there he would have traveled to California and boarded a steamship for the ten-day trip to Honolulu.

We don't know where Wesley lived or how he was employed in Hawaii. Public records show that he married Madeline Kahaleuluohia Lazarus on April 8, 1922, in Honolulu. Madeline was employed as a stenographer and living alone. She was twenty-eight years old, and Wesley was forty-three. Given his experience as an accountant, Wesley surely would have found a job somewhere in the city.

Madeline was a native Hawaiian, born in 1893, and identified as "Black/Hawaiian" in the 1900 census. Her parents were native Hawaiians: her father, Eleazar Lazarus, was born in 1860, ninety-nine years before Hawaii was to become a state, and her mother, Julia, in 1868. Both Eleazar and Julia died young, leaving their children orphans. Julia died of bronchitis when she was age twenty-nine, and four months later, Eleazar, thirty-seven, died of consumption. Madeline was four years old, and her brother just two.

Madeline and her brother were taken in by their paternal grandmother, Kauimakaole Lazarus, who was a difficult and unstable woman. She divorced her husband in 1893 and then spent years involved in acrimonious litigation, first with her husband over alimony payments, and then with her son over their respective rights to property in her husband's estate after his death. Various other suits featured members of the family fighting each other, and as one judge wrote, "the Lazarus family has ever been at enmity with itself." When Madeline was nine, her grandmother petitioned the court for a guardian to be appointed for the two young children, though no resolution of the petition was recorded. Madeline's grandmother died in 1908, when Madeline was fifteen. There's no record of where Madeline and her brother lived until they could be on their own.

Eleazer Jr. married before his sister. In 1918, he named his first daughter Madeline. Soon after his sister's marriage in 1922, Eleazer had a son and named him Wesley after his new brother-in-law.

We know very little about Wesley and Madeline over the next years. For some period, they lived with her brother, his wife, and their five children. Steamship records show that Wesley and Madeline made several trips back and forth between Honolulu and Wilmington, California, a port located in a section of Los Angeles County, near Long Beach.

Wesley kept in touch with Georgianna and Pearl, and he and Madeline visited them in St. Paul. A photograph, likely taken in St. Paul in the late 1920s and sent to us by Pearl's daughter, shows Wesley and Madeline with Georgianna and Pearl and two unidentified persons. The group is standing in front of a Buick, and they are all facing the camera. Georgianna stands next to Madeline.

Pictured from left to right: unidentified man, Madeline Lazarus Elkins, Georgianna Dowden Ellis, unidentified woman, Wesley Elkins, Pearl Ellis. The photo was likely taken in the late 1920s. (Courtesy of Marilyn Hernwall.)

Wesley and Pearl are at the far right, smiling and standing close together with their arms affectionately around each other's shoulders. In this picture, Pearl is as tall as Wesley.

IN 1928, Pearl married Carl Hernwall in St. Paul, and the couple moved to Jacksonville, Florida. Shortly after that, Georgianna sold the house on Ashland Avenue—the one that Wesley had purchased more than two decades earlier—and joined her daughter in Florida.

When Wesley and Madeline traveled to California, it seems likely that they were looking for a place to live. In 1928, they left Hawaii and her family and settled in Fontana, California, in San Bernardino County.

Fontana had been founded in 1913 and quickly became a thriving agricultural center. Farmers in the area formed the Fontana Citrus Growers Association and planted acres of citrus fruit. By 1920, the largest individual citrus orchard in the world—5,000 acres—was located in Fontana. Other crops also flourished: peanuts, barley, sweet potatoes, and soon grapes. In 1925, it claimed the largest hog farm in the world. Rabbits were raised and bred. A huge poultry processing plant was constructed.

The region was blessed with a climate that was different from what Wesley had experienced in the Midwest. For most of the year, the days were filled with bright sunshine and were seldom overcast or cold. It never snowed. Summers could be hot, but it was a dry heat instead of the hot and muggy summer weather in Iowa and Minnesota. There were no mosquitoes, and flowers bloomed year-round. In the fall, the stiff Santa Ana winds started up in the high desert east of the mountains. The winds swept over the San Bernardino Mountains, rushing toward the coast, blowing hot dry clouds of dust across the landscape.

When World War II came, the shipbuilder Henry J. Kaiser built a steel plant in Fontana that produced material for the war effort. Men quit their jobs in the citrus and poultry industries and went to work in the steel factory. More than four months after Pearl Harbor, in late April 1942, Wesley was required to register once again for the draft. He was sixty-three years old. For men in Wesley's age category, it was called the "Old Man's Draft," and if asked to serve, these men would have been assigned to nonmilitary jobs.

In the last years of her life, Madeline worked as a stenographer at Norton Air Force Base. Wesley was listed in the published phone directories of the 1950s as John W. Elkins.

The couple lived in a house on a small lot at 9185 Pepper Street. Like many of his neighbors, Wesley raised chickens. Standing in his front yard and looking up the street to the east, he had a clear view of the San Bernardino Mountains, snowcapped in winter, a dusty brown and green in the summer.

Madeline died of heart disease and a pulmonary embolism on March 12, 1959. She was sixty-five years old and had been married to Wesley for thirty-seven years. They had no children. Madeline was buried on a grassy hillside in the Montecito Cemetery in Colton, California.

In the last two years of his life, Wesley Elkins had a public guardian, suggesting that he had physical or mental problems preventing him from taking care of himself. He died on March 7, 1961. The death certificate listed his occupation as "Poultryman," in the business of "ranching, poultry." His birthplace was noted as Clayton County, Iowa. Heart disease was the cause of death.

The *San Bernardino Sun* ran a three-sentence obituary: "John Wesley Elkins, 81, of 9185 Pepper Street, Fontana, died Tuesday in a San Bernardino hospital. A native of Iowa, he had lived in Fontana 33 years. Services are pending at Stanley Dickey Mortuary, Fontana."

A few days later, Wesley Elkins was buried next to his wife in the Montecito Cemetery.

WESLEY ELKINS rarely talked about his difficult childhood and never blamed others for the crime he committed as an eleven-year-old boy. He acknowledged his responsibility for what transpired in the early morning of July 17, 1889, and expressed his sorrow and remorse. In prison, he took Warden Barr's words to heart, believing that he could win his freedom by adhering to the rules of the institution and developing his intellect. He succeeded in educating himself, and he excelled at writing and, later at Cornell Academy, in public speaking. He won the backing of prominent Iowans—educators, politicians, newspaper editors—who championed the cause of his freedom. His life's path was guided by his primary mentor, Professor James Harlan of Cornell College. When Wesley left Anamosa Penitentiary, he continued his education until he joined the workforce. After that, he remained steadily employed, reconnected with and supported family members, and maintained a successful marriage for nearly four decades.

The account of Wesley Elkins' life is a story of redemption. He proved himself in the adult world and kept the promise he made in his letter to Iowa legislators after he was granted a conditional parole in April 1902. Although we have quoted parts of the letter before, the last paragraph is worth reading in full:

I will go out from these walls with a moral certainty that I have many warm earnest friends who are intensely interested in my well being. This fact to my mind is valuable beyond expression. To you and to others who contributed in any way, by voice or vote towards securing favorable action, I extend my sincere and heartfelt thanks, and to those who at present are opposed I appeal to them to withhold their judgment until I have time to demonstrate outside of these walls whether my pretensions of leading a life upright in character, strong and thoughtful, gentlemanly always, are genuine or false, and I can confidently believe at the end of ten years they will hasten to commend the action of the Twenty-Ninth General Assembly of Iowa.

Very respectfully and gratefully, Wesley Elkins

EPILOGUE

IN ORDER TO accurately tell the story of Wesley Elkins, we did extensive research. Primary sources were vital to our understanding as we sought to map the trajectory of his life. We read newspaper accounts of the crime and transcripts of the inquest and the Grand Jury hearing. Legislative records helped us follow the progress of his appeals, and we had access to statehouse reports. We studied prison records, state and county histories, and archival materials stored at state historical societies in Iowa and Minnesota. To trace the complicated family trees, we relied on census records and other public documents. We were fortunate to have many of the published and unpublished letters Wesley wrote from prison and during the ten years after he was released.

We didn't find answers to every question that arose during our research. James Corlett continued to press his claim to the $500 reward offered by the state for the arrest and conviction of the murderer of John and Hattie Elkins. After he initially applied to outgoing Governor Larrabee for the reward and was rebuffed, he wrote to the new governor, Horace Boies, in May 1890. Two months later, Corlett submitted a sworn statement from Sheriff Kann relating the facts leading up to Wesley's arrest as the sheriff remembered them. Kann stated that he believed that Corlett was entitled to the reward. Boies replied that "From my present understanding of the facts in regard to the Elkins reward, I do not think it was ever earned by anyone." Corlett tried again in May 1895, writing to Governor Jackson, noting that he now also had the support of former Governor Larrabee. We did not find proof that the reward was ever paid.

Perhaps most significantly, we don't know what happened to the infant—Nellie Elkins—who was in the bed with her parents when they were killed. Possibly she was taken in or adopted by a family in the community, and her name was changed. One report, which we could not confirm, suggested that she died in infancy, but we could find no official notice of her death.

We can complete the stories of some of the individuals who played significant roles in the drama of John Wesley Elkins.

Cora Bassett, Wesley's older half-sister, had been married to George Bassett for forty-one years when he died at the age of sixty-three in 1927. Cora lived another twenty years, until she was eighty-seven years old. According to her obituary in 1957, she was survived by her brother Wesley in California, three sons, and "four grandchildren, twelve great-grandchildren, six great-great grandchildren and a host of friends."

Wesley's half-brother, Mark Elkins, and his wife, Lottie, had one son, Elmer, when Wesley visited Minnesota in 1903. Three years later, the couple had a daughter, who they named Nellie. She suffered from epilepsy and spent most of her life in institutions— the State Epileptic Farm and then the Hospital for Epileptics and School for the Feeble Minded in Boone County, Iowa. She died in her late twenties. Mark continued to live in Minnesota, close to his sister and her family. He divorced and remarried, worked on farms and then, later, as a foreman at a meat packing plant. He died at the age of seventy-five in 1947. He is buried with his second wife, Alice, in Delaware County, Iowa.

Susan Glaspell, the young Iowa writer who was inspired by Wesley's struggle for freedom and wrote the short story known today as "The Plea," became one of America's most popular and well-regarded writers of the first half of the twentieth century. Her two most famous works are frequently anthologized and considered classics of American literature: the one-act play *Trifles*, written in 1916, and the short story "A Jury of Her Peers," adapted from the play and written the following year. Glaspell published short stories, novels, plays, and a biography. She cofounded the

Provincetown Players, mentored Eugene O'Neill, and won the Pulitzer Prize for Drama in 1931. Glaspell died in 1948 at the age of seventy-two.

Three wardens, all of whom supported Wesley's bid for freedom, supervised him at Anamosa Penitentiary. Marquis Barr, the warden who first encouraged Wesley, left his position in 1892 and took a position as a claims agent with the Minneapolis, St. Paul, and Sault Ste. Marie Railroad. Barr later returned to Anamosa to serve another stint as warden from 1906 to 1911. He died in 1923. His obituary praised him for using "methods of persuasion and patience and kindness" in dealing with prisoners, and for his commitment to "the uplifting work of giving the prisoner the chance to make good."

Philander Madden left Anamosa in 1898 amid serious charges of mismanagement. During his short tenure, he was a significant influence on Wesley Elkins, encouraging him, helping him to attract supporters, and recognizing his intellectual abilities. Wesley visited Warden Madden after he was released from prison to express his gratitude in person. Madden served as the city jailer for Des Moines and died in 1913. He was characterized as a "caring and compassionate man" who was "generous to a fault."

William Hunter succeeded Madden and oversaw the release of Wesley in 1902. As warden, Hunter made significant improvements in the lives of the prisoners at Anamosa and was praised as "a leading light among prison reformers," leaving behind "an institution which has been termed by experts in this line to be the model of its kind in the United States." He was sixty-one years old, still serving as warden of Anamosa, when he died of Bright's disease in 1906.

Five governors were involved in Wesley's bids for pardon and parole.

Wesley addressed his first appeal to Governor Frank Jackson in 1895. Although Jackson was due to leave office the following year, he agreed to forward it to the General Assembly. After his single term in office, Jackson resumed his position as president of an insurance company and died in 1938 at the age of eighty-four.

Francis Drake was serving as governor in the spring of 1896, when the House and Senate Committees on Penitentiaries and Pardons rejected Wesley's application. Wesley's appeal was not discussed on the floor of the capitol, and it did not reach the governor's desk. In 1897, two months before he stepped down, Drake chose to forward Wesley's second appeal to the General Assembly. Drake was a single-term governor, a distinguished citizen of Iowa, well known as a lawyer, banker, and railroad magnate. He founded and endowed Drake University and served as President of the Board of Trustees. He died in 1903 at the age of seventy-two.

Leslie Shaw served as governor for two terms. Although he had refused to forward Wesley's appeal to the General Assembly in 1899—going against the advice of his friend, Professor Harlan—he sent it on in 1901, a move that led to Wesley's parole the next spring. After stepping down as governor, Shaw succeeded in his goal to work in the federal government. A skilled orator and expert on issues of banking and finance, he was involved in the creation of the Federal Reserve System. In 1902, President Theodore Roosevelt picked Shaw to be his Secretary of the Treasury, and Shaw continued in that position for five years. He died in 1932 at the age of eighty-three.

Albert Cummins was also a man of great ambition and political accomplishment. Cummins was the first Iowa governor to serve three terms, and during his time as governor, from 1902 until 1908, he received the monthly reports from Wesley. Cummins was later chosen to represent Iowa in the U.S. Senate, serving in that capacity from 1908 until his death in July 1926 at the age of seventy-six. Cummins ran back-to-back campaigns for the Republican nomination for president in 1912 and 1916, and, although he wasn't chosen as the party's nominee, he served as president pro tempore of the Senate from 1919 to 1925.

Beryl Carroll, the sitting governor when Wesley was released from Anamosa Penitentiary, served four years as the state's chief executive. During his tenure as governor, he was once "hailed as a hero for entering a burning building in Des Moines and retrieving a trunk containing valuable property." After leaving the governorship, Carroll worked in the life insurance business. He died at the age of seventy-nine in 1939.

William P. Whipple was the state senator who was the principal advocate for Wesley's release. As chairman of the Senate Committee on Penitentiaries and Pardons, Whipple argued vigorously for Wesley's parole during the 1902 legislative session. We know from Wesley's letters that he stayed in contact with Whipple in the years after his release. *The History of Benton County, Iowa*, published in 1910, the year of the senator's death, notes that Whipple was a man who "had the courage of his convictions" and that he gave "careful and painstaking consideration [to the] noted Wesley Elkins case."

Carl Snyder, who brought Wesley to the attention of the public in Iowa, became a prominent national figure. Before Wesley was released, Snyder moved to New York City, where he pursued a career as a journalist and writer. He lectured and published extensively, notably on topics related to economics and statistics. For years, he worked in the research department of the Federal Reserve Bank of New York. He also served as President of the American Statistical Association. Later in his life, he moved to Santa Barbara, California, only 150 miles west of where Wesley lived in Fontana. We do not know if Snyder and Wesley met or communicated in the years they both lived on the West Coast.

In 1960, fourteen years after Carl Snyder died, his wife, Madeline Raisch, established the Carl Snyder Memorial Lecture Series at the University of California at Santa Barbara. More than twenty Nobel Prize winners in Economics have lectured in this series. The list of Nobel laureates includes such well-known economists as Paul Samuelson, Milton Friedman, and Paul Krugman.

James Harlan, the Cornell College professor who was one of Wesley's earliest supporters, devoted more time and energy to his case than anyone else. Professor Harlan maintained contact with Wesley for many years, visiting him several times in St. Paul. Harlan was connected to Cornell College for more than sixty years in a variety of capacities: as a professor; vice president; president from 1908 to 1914; and member of the Board of Trustees. Harlan's house on the campus was acquired by the college in 1934, a year after his death, and the building has been used as a residence or meeting place for faculty and students for many years.

Professor James Harlan died in 1933, at the age of eighty-eight. He and his wife, Janette, had been married for sixty-four years. William Boyd, the former editor of the *Cedar Rapids Republican,* wrote a eulogy for Professor Harlan, describing Harlan's support of Wesley: how Harlan had fought for Wesley's parole, given him a home, and encouraged his education. Boyd remembered how persuasive Harlan was in making the case for Wesley.

> Years ago, a little boy, warped by influences for which he was not to blame—so Doctor Harlan thought—committed a shocking crime. . . . One day I read of a movement to secure for him a pardon, which at that time required a formal act of the legislature. Carelessly, as editors too often do, I wrote a paragraph to the effect that the interests of society, as well as those of the boy himself, would probably be best served if he remained where he was.
>
> A day or two later a letter came to me from Doctor Harlan saying that he thought if I had looked into that case as he had, I would not have written that paragraph. Would I not go with him to the prison, meet the youth, study the data he had gathered, and then see if I would not reverse judgment?
>
> Anyone who would have turned a deaf ear to Doctor Harlan's appeal would have been unworthy of his friendship. I went. I reversed judgment, and, with others, became Doctor Harlan's ally.

Boyd's tribute also noted that Harlan's relationship with Wesley "reveals the heart of the man, its tenderness; its quality of mercy guided by wisdom which never led to misplaced confidence."

AS WE WORKED on this project, we traveled to many of the locations where John Wesley Elkins lived throughout his life. Years had passed since Wesley was present there, and we wanted to see these places for ourselves.

We drove through rural Clayton County to the location of the small house on Bear Creek where Wesley had killed his parents; that structure was torn down long ago. We visited the downtown area of Elkader. During our trip to Elkader, we interviewed a retired Clayton County deputy sheriff and investigator. We asked him if he knew the story of John Wesley Elkins. He said he did, and then referred to Wesley as "that little bastard who killed his parents," expressing the same opinion of Wesley that county residents held 130 years earlier.

We toured Anamosa State Penitentiary. Authorities did not show us the exact cell Wesley occupied, although they told us that the inside of the prison had changed very little since Wesley was incarcerated more than a century ago.

In St. Paul, we saw the apartment building near Summit Avenue where Wesley lived in his first weeks in the city, and later, we parked in front of the house on Ashland Avenue that Wesley so proudly purchased in 1909. The neighborhood appears quiet and family oriented. Except for the modern cars on the street, the area looks as it must have when Wesley lived there—the houses close together, the lots deep, the lawns and street shaded by overhanging tree branches. Most of the houses have flower boxes or plantings in the front; many have gardens in the back. Young children ride bicycles in the street.

The town of Fontana, California, where Wesley lived with his wife for the last three decades of his life, is a bustling city today.

Their old neighborhood is located a few blocks from the more crowded areas of business and traffic. It is peaceful on Pepper Street, and people still raise chickens in their yards. In the early morning, the sun rises over the San Bernardino Mountains, and roosters crow to announce the dawn of a new day.

ACKNOWLEDGMENTS

WE ARE DEEPLY indebted to Steve Wendl and the late Richard "Dick" Snavely (1946–2018), former employees of the Anamosa State Penitentiary, for introducing us to the story of John Wesley Elkins and for their numerous and substantial contributions to our research. We communicated with them many times as we worked on this book. They guided us on a tour of the inside of the facility, responded to our frequent questions, provided us with additional source material, and directed us to the Anamosa State Penitentiary Prison History website (www.asphistory.com). Thanks to Steve and Dick, a detailed record of the institution has been preserved on the website and is accessible to visitors. The website contains historical background, information about prison wardens, hundreds of photographs, and many remarkable stories of inmates and prison life over the years.

We did much of our research at the State Historical Society of Iowa in Des Moines, and we are particularly grateful to Gordon Hendrickson, former State Archivist, who made the decision to give us access to the Governor's Correspondence on Criminal Matters. Those boxes contained relevant legal documents, including transcripts of the Coroner's Inquest and the Grand Jury hearing, as well as numerous unpublished letters written by Wesley Elkins and others.

Other staff members at the Historical Society, including Jeffrey Dawson, Sharon Avery, Rosie Springer, and Shari Stelling, were generous with their time and helped us to find valuable primary source material stored in the archives. Biennial Reports of the Warden of the Penitentiary at Anamosa, with the Reports of the Officers of the Institution, to the Governor of Iowa, 1873–1907, supplied statistics and details about prison life. Legislative Records of the General Assembly, including Journals of the House and Senate, furnished critical information about the legislative debates.

We are grateful to Marvin Bergman, former editor of the *Annals of Iowa*, who offered insightful editorial comments on Patricia's article "John Wesley Elkins, Boy Murderer, and His Struggle for Pardon," which was published in the *Annals* in summer 2010. Specific citations for some of the facts and quotations in this book may be found in that article. Thanks also to Andrew Klumpp, current editor of the *Annals*. Patricia's work was supported, in part, by a grant from the State Historical Society of Iowa.

The papers of James Harlan are stored in the Cole Library at Cornell College in Mount Vernon, Iowa, and we appreciated the assistance of staff members who gave us access to that material. Thanks are also due to Meghan Yamanishi, the archivist at Cole Library, for providing the photographs of Wesley Elkins and the Gladstone Literary Society.

In gathering information for this book, we relied on numerous sources listed in the bibliography. Details of the riot at the Mitchellville Girls School came from contemporary newspaper accounts, as well as "Susan Glaspell's 'Plea' for Juvenile Justice," by Marcia Noe and Holly Hill, and "Savage Girls: The 1899 Riot at the Mitchellville Girls School," by Sharon E. Wood.

The portion of Chapter 21 that describes the release of Wesley Elkins is based on an article by Frank Moorhead that appeared in the *Des Moines Daily Capital* on April 19, 1902.

Chapter 25 explores the origins and themes of Susan Glaspell's short story, "In the Face of His Constituents" (later retitled "The Plea"), which was inspired by the legislative debate over the granting of a conditional parole to Wesley Elkins. Some of the material in this chapter is directly sourced from Patricia's article "Foreshadowing 'A Jury of Her Peers': Susan Glaspell's 'The Plea' and the Case of John Wesley Elkins," published in 2008 in *Susan Glaspell: New Directions in Critical Inquiry*.

To research the years that Wesley Elkins lived in St. Paul, we reviewed additional information at the Minnesota Historical Society. We relied on newspaper articles, census records, land records, steamship records, and other public documents to complete the story of Wesley Elkins after he left St. Paul in 1920.

In writing this book, we have been scrupulous in staying true to the historical facts. All of the scenes are based on primary sources, and we have quoted from these materials throughout the book. In quoted passages, we have occasionally made minor changes in spelling, punctuation, or wording for the sake of consistency or readability. These changes do not affect the original meaning of the text.

Finally, we should note three websites that proved to be particularly useful in our research: Ancestry.com; NewspaperArchive .com; and Newspapers.com.

WE OWE THANKS to Eric Mennel and Phoebe Judge for publicizing the story of Wesley Elkins to a national audience on the NPR podcast, *Criminal*. The episode aired on February 15, 2015, and can be found at http://thisiscriminal.com/https://www.google.com/ search?client=firefox-b-1-d&q=criminal+podcast+wesley+Elkins.

Patricia's talented research assistants provided crucial assistance in our investigation of this crime and its aftermath. Ben Iddings, Taylor Browne, Morgan Stoddard, Kindra Bradley, Kafiya Bello, David Herring, Rachel Rogers, Michael Stanley, Ashley Arthur, and Allyn Sharp, all made important contributions. Thanks also to Nick Sexton for his friendship and responsiveness to our inquiries.

For providing additional information about Wesley Elkins, we want to acknowledge Ilo Rhines, Judy Moyna, and Betty Rogers.

A special thank you to Marilyn Hernwall, who generously provided us with family photographs and stories of her relatives, Georgianna Dowden Ellis and Pearl Ellis Hernwall. We also appreciated information about the family from Lee Dorothy, Kathy Lemire, and Ted Brooks.

Several fellow writers, including Marjorie Hudson, Philip Gerard, and Don Knefel, contributed to our work by reading portions of the manuscript and offering suggestions. Steve Wendl reviewed and commented on "The Prison Years," the part of the book dealing with the history of Anamosa State Penitentiary.

Thanks especially to Dave Shaw for his careful reading and editorial suggestions on the penultimate draft of the manuscript.

For residencies where parts of this book were written, Tom wishes to thank Jim Roberts and Deborah Jakubs of Doe Branch Ink and Katrina Denza of the Weymouth Center for the Arts.

Patricia appreciated the steadfast support of former deans of the University of North Carolina School of Law, including Judith Wegner, Gene Nichol, and Jack Boger, and current dean, Martin Brinkley. Patricia acknowledges that her work was funded, in part, by a grant from the North Carolina Law Center Foundation.

We were fortunate to have the support of the University of Iowa Press. Catherine Cocks encouraged Patricia's work in the early phases. Jim McCoy and Bill Friedricks provided editorial oversight and assistance. Special thanks, too, to Tegan Daly, Karen Copp, and Allison Means for their contributions. We also wish to acknowledge Daniel Forrest-Bank, who did a meticulous job as our copyeditor.

And finally, we want to thank family members—Carol and Ted Ballou, Julie Bosworth, Carol and Des Runyan, John and Grace Wolf, Michael Wolf, and David Wolf—who encouraged us over the years as we worked to tell the story of Wesley Elkins.

SELECTED BIBLIOGRAPHY

Newspaper Sources

We relied extensively on local newspapers for information about the crime, the legal proceedings, and the legislative debates. Many of our descriptions of scenes, people, and events came from newspaper accounts, and we've often noted in the text where the article appeared. Specific citations can be found in Patricia's article in the *Annals of Iowa* cited below.

The newspapers we consulted include, among many others: *Anamosa Eureka; Anamosa Journal; Anamosa Prison Press*; *Cedar Falls Gazette; Cedar Rapids Gazette; Cedar Rapids Republican; Clayton County Centennial; Clayton County Democrat; Council Bluffs Nonpareil; Davenport Republican*; *Des Moines Daily Capital*; *Des Moines Daily Leader*; *Des Moines Daily News*; *Dubuque Daily Times; Dubuque Herald; Elkader Argus; Elkader Register*; *Mount Vernon Hawkeye*; *Semi-Weekly Iowa State Reporter*.

Additional Sources

Ambrose, Stephen E. *Nothing Like It in the World: The Men Who Built the Transcontinental Railroad 1863–1869*. New York: Simon and Schuster, 2000.

Ben-Zvi, Linda. *Susan Glaspell: Her Life and Times*. New York: Oxford University Press, 2005.

Blomberg, Thomas G., and Karol Lucken. *American Penology: A History of Control*. 2nd ed. New Brunswick, NJ: Transaction Publishers, 2010.

Boyd, William R. "James Elliott Harlan, 1845–1933," *Cornell College Bulletin* 35, no. 8 (1934).

Briggs, John E. *History of Social Legislation in Iowa*. Iowa City, IA: State University of Iowa, 1915.

Bryan, Patricia L. "Foreshadowing 'A Jury of Her Peers': Susan Glaspell's 'The Plea' and the Case of John Wesley Elkins," In *Susan Glaspell: New Directions in Critical Inquiry*. Edited by Martha Carpentier. Cambridge, MA: Cambridge Scholars Publishing, 2008.

———. "John Wesley Elkins, Boy Murderer, and His Struggle for Pardon," *Annals of Iowa* 69, No. 3 (2010): 261–307.

Burgstahler, H. J. "James Elliott Harlan, 1845–1933," *Cornell College Bulletin* 35, no. 8 (1934).

Cole, Cyrenus. *A History of the People of Iowa*. Cedar Rapids, IA: Torch Press, 1921.

Curtis, Charles. *Five Years at Anamosa*. Published by the author, 1899.

English, Emory. "Pioneer Lawmakers Honored." *Annals of Iowa* 31 (1951): 1–35.

Finn, Bertha. *Anamosa, A Reminiscence: 1838–1938*. Anamosa: Anamosa Historical Society, 1988.

Fraker, Fleming, Jr. "The Beginnings of the Progressive Movement in Iowa," *Annals of Iowa* 35 (1961): 34–60.

Garvy, George. "Carl Snyder, Pioneer Economic Statistician and Monetarist," *History of Political Economy* 10.3 (1978): 455–490.

Glaspell, Susan. *Her America: "A Jury of Her Peers" and Other Stories*. Edited by Patricia L. Bryan and Martha Carpentier, introduction by the editors. Iowa City: University of Iowa Press, 2010.

———. "In the Face of His Constituents," *Harper's Magazine*, October 1903.

———. "The Plea," in *Lifted Masks*. New York: 1912.

Haynes, Fred E. *The Iowa Prison System*. Iowa City: State University of Iowa, 1954.

Heywood, C. William. *Cornell College: A Sesquicentennial History, 1853–2003*. Cedar Rapids, IA: WDG Publishing, 2004.

Hillis, Hazel. "Securing the Juvenile Court Law in Iowa," *Annals of Iowa* 23 (1942): 161–188.

Kean, A. W. G. "The History of the Criminal Liability of Children," *Law Q. Review* 53 (1937).

Koons, E. Wade. "Wesley Elkins," *Coe College Courier*, December 12, 1899.

Martin, Albro. *James J. Hill and the Opening of the Midwest*. Reprint edition. Introduction by W. Thomas White. St. Paul, MN: Minnesota Historical Society Press (1991).

McKay, Joyce. "Reforming Prisoners and Prisons: Iowa's State Prisons—The First 100 Years," *Annals of Iowa* 60 (2001): 139–173.

McKelvey, Blake. *American Prisons: A History of Good Intentions*. Montclair, NJ: Patterson and Smith, 1977.